HARYANA
A Historical Perspective

S. C. Mittal

PUBLISHERS & DISTRIBUTORS (P) LTD

7/22, Ansari Road, Darya Ganj, New Delhi
Tel.: +91-11-4077 5252, 2327 3880
E-mail: orders@atlanticbooks.com
Web: www.atlanticbooks.com

Reprint 2026

Published by Atlantic Publishers & Distributors (P) Ltd.

Printed & bound in India by Atlantic Print Services

Preface

The present study is a dispassionate and systematic attempt at a reconstruction of the historical past of Haryana. It deals with events from those following the Third Battle of Panipat to the formation of the new State of Haryana in 1966. The work examines the nature of political ideas, institutions and the course of struggle of the people of Haryana in a historical perspective, and in doing so analyses the character of the political structure of Haryana under the local chiefs, the East India Company and the British Crown.

It raises and answers the pertinent questions as: to why this region could not gain a separate political and administrative identity earlier, and was tagged to Delhi (1803), North-Western Provinces (1834), or the Punjab (1858). Besides it explores why the growth of national consciousness was stunted in this region and the Indian National Congress could not strike deep roots here.

This study meticulously describes the nature of mutual rivalries and conflict among the local chiefs and the changing attitude of the British Residents and Governor-Generals towards them. Its important concern comprises the study of the wider impact of the 1857 uprisings, the socio-religious reform movements of the later nineteenth century, the contribution of Haryana during the First World War, the nature, character and course of the national movement in the region up to the Indian Independence, the subsequent sufferings of the Punjab people and their migration with all its aftermath, and the demand for a separate state and its formation in 1966.

Having had no separate administrative identity for a long period, Haryana has received scant attention at the hands of historians. There are hardly any books available on the subject. Whatever books have been published are of a very general nature and most of the available books on the region, whether official or non-official, generally give one-sided version of things.

Regional history often draws an insufficient line between what is regional and what is general (*i.e.*, national), and frequently, because of its main concern with a particular region, it tends to become parochial. However, in this study care has been taken to provide a broader convas to regional events and problems, thereby examining them in an all-India setting. Thus, the present study attempts to fill a gap in the history of regional studies by providing a comprehensive and balanced treatment of historical issues.

This study is based on a fairly large number of sources—the files of Home and Foreign Departments of Government of India, some relevant office records, including proceedings of Parliamentary debates, memoirs, private papers, diaries, and autobiographics (published and unpublished). Moreover, research journals and leading newspapers have been extensively tapped.

I owe a deep debt of gratitude to Professor V.N. Datta for his sustained encouragement. I am also thankful to Professor K.C. Yadav whose books in the field stimulated me to further study of the history of Haryana region. I am extremely grateful to my friend and colleague Dr. G. Khurana for his valuable suggestions. My thanks are due to the Directors of the National Archives and Nehru Museum and Library, New Delhi, the Librarians of the libraries of Punjab University, Chandigarh, Punjabi University, Patiala, and of Dwarka Das Library, Chandigarh, and Kurukshetra University, Kurukshetra. I am also thankful to Parmod, my wife, and Vandana, my daughter, who gave me invaluable help in preparing the index and completing the book.

Kurukshetra University,
Kurukshetra **S.C. Mittal**
15th October, 1985.

Contents

1

Haryana and its Changing Masters (1761-1803)

Since the invasion of Nadirshah Delhi and its environs had been the paradise of freebooters and the people of this area had suffered heavily and faced severe hardships and agony. In continuation of the plundering activity by the Marathas and the Afghans, now in the later half of the 18th century, it had become the looting ground of the Sikhs, the Rohilla chiefs, and the foreign adventurers. In fact, the Third Battle of Panipat did not decide the fate of the people of Haryana. Though the Maratha melted and the Afghans retired,[1] it left the field for the new masters *i.e.* the Jats, the Sikhs, the Rohillas, the Marathas and the Europeans who were engaged into their mutual rivalries and conflicts.

Ahmad Shah Abdali after looting Delhi and the adjoining territories of Haryana for two and half months left it on 20th March, 1761. He appointed Najib-ud-duala the *de facto* ruler of Delhi,[2] who kept in his possession the Southern Haryana upto Panipat.[3] Zaina Khan, the Governor of Sarhind, was given the northern part of Haryana, including the territories of Karnal, Thanesar, Ambala and Jind districts.[4] The remaining portion of Haryana continued to be as a part of the Mughal kingdom. Though Ahmad Shah Abdali recognised Shah Alam II (1759-1806) as Emperor, Imad-ul-duala as *Vazir* and Najib or Najib-ud-duala as *Mir Bakhshi*, it was the latter[5] who virtually ruled over the kingdom for about ten years (1761-1770).

Rise of Jats

The people of Haryana did not reconcile themselves to the new set up. The Jats of Haryana were the first to revolt Najib-ud-duala made tremendous efforts to control Haryana territories in order to keep his domination at Delhi intact. He went towards Hansi-Hissar to subdue the rebels but the main opposition came from the Jats of Bharatpur who were being led by Suraj Mal.

In order to know the actual situation it is necessary to briefly examine the circumstances which led to the emergence of Suraj Mal as a force to reckon with. The rivalry between the Jats of Bharatpur and Mughal rulers of Delhi was not a new thing. In fact, the Jats played a prominent role in the disintegration of the Mughal empire and stiff opposition to Ahmad Shah Abdali.[6] They protested against the Mughal emperors as early as the time of Aurangzeb, the religious bigotry and economic extortions being the chief irritants.[7] Their leaders were Gokala (1669), Raja Ram (1668), Bhajja Singh (1688-95), Churaman (1695-1721) and Badan Singh (1772-1756).

The establishment of the Jat State of Bharatpur was a 'political upheaval of the first magnitude.'[8] Suraj Mal (1756-63), the adopted son of Badan Singh, was one of the ablest statesmen and warriors.[9] Though he was uneducated he was the 'Plato of the Jats.'[10] To Jadunath Sarkar he was the shrewdest Hindu potentate then alive.[11] K.R. Qanungo calls him the 'Jat ulysses.'[12]

Suraj Mal made his mark even before being the real ruler. Ahmad Shah (1748-54) and Alamgir II (1754-59), the Mughal rulers, were perturbed by the rising powers of Chaudhry Balram of Ballabhgarh and of Suraj Mal. The latter helped Balram many times, against the Mughals. However, in 1753 Balram was executed by the Mughals. Suraj Mal could not tolerate this insult. He threatened the Mughal *Vazir* to rectum the *Jagir* of Balram to his two sons. Consequently, Kishan Singh, the elder son of Balram was appointed the *Qiledar* and Hira Singh, the younger son as *Nazim*, and Suraj Mal himself became their patron. In fact, he was one of the greatest figures of his times—great both in war and diplomacy. Under him the Jats spread beyond the Yamuna, and came to possess the whole of Mewat.[13] However, neither the Mughals nor the Afghans approved of the increasing power of Suraj Mal. The latter soon became the undisputed leader of the Jats. He was the man who enlarged a small territory of his domination into a small kingdom. He proved to be a staunch enemy of both the Mughals and the Afghans.

Earlier, Ahmad Shah (1748-54), the Mughal ruler, sent Malhar Rao Holkar and Jai Appa Sindhia, the Maratha generals, to subdue Suraj Mal. In the battle, Khande Rao, the son of Malhar Rao Holkar was killed in action.[14] Anyhow, the fortress of Dig of the Jats was taken with the help of artillery.[15]

Ahmad Shah Abdali also found Suraj Mal as a great obstacle in his way. During his fourth invasion in 1759, Ahmad Shah sent some of his troops under Firuz Jang against Suraj Mal and himself followed the army. After snatching the fort of Ballabhgarh, Abdali sent an army to Mathura which massacred and looted the pilgrims.[16] But due to a dreadful pestilence which broke out with great virulence in his army[17] Ahmad Shah was compelled to abandon his intention of chastising Suraj Mal,[18] and retreated to Kabul. Later, according to *Tarikh-i-Ibratnama,* Imad-ul-duala, the rebellious *Vazir* due to fear his own life, saw no other means of safety than in seeking the protection of Suraj Mal and fled and took refuge with him.[19]

Despite several intrigues and insults by the Marathas, Suraj Mal promised all the help to the Marathas against Ahmad Shah Abdali. But he was soon disillusioned with the Marathas, withdrew in disgust from the Maratha camp and returned to Ballabhgarh. Perhaps this withdrawal might have been caused by his differences with Sadhashiv Bhau, the Commander-in-Chief of the Maratha forces, over the strategy to be followed and some Personal prejudices or dislikes for the Maratha supremacy.[20] Suraj Mal favoured some sort of guerilla warfare while Bhau resolved to fight a pitched battle. Possibly Suraj Mal was justified in his assessment of the strategy due to geographical situation and experience.[21] But for the second reason it was due to the arrogance and folly of Bhau.[22] Perhaps Suraj Mal protested against Maratha vandalism in Delhi palace and dissuaded Bhau from going to Kunjpura.[23] Bhau regarded Suraj Mal as a petty landed chief not accustomed to affairs on a grand scale.[24] However, Suraj Mal remained liberal towards the Marathas. He gave asylum to a large number of defeated Maratha soldiers.

The defeat of the Marathas in Panipat provided an oppor tunity for Suraj Mal to extend his kingdom. He attempted to capture large parts of Haryana. He occupied Agra, the richest city in the Empire and paid a tribute of one lakh to Ahmad Shah Abdali, which he willingly accepted. In the Doab Suraj Mal now occupied several Maratha *jagirs* and recovered his earlier possession. He sent Jawahir Singh, his son to attack on Musavi Khan, the Mughal *faujdar* of Gurgaon and Rohtak. He himself followed the army. Musavi Khan was arrested and Farrukhnagar, the Headquarters of Musavi Khan was captured by Suraj Mal in December 1763. He also conquered the territories of Pataudi, Rewari and Rohtak. He also repulsed the attack of Bhadur Khan, the Beloch leader of Bahadurgarh, who was defeated and his territory was also occupied.

Najib-ud-duala was alarmed by the increasing power of Suraj Mal and demanded the immediate release of Musavi Khan. Suraj Mal accepted Najib-ud-duala's demand. However, Najib-ud-duala attacked Suraj Mal and killed him in a battle near the river Hinden on December 25, 1763.[25] His death was a great loss to the Jats. In fact he was the man who was loved by Jats, respected by his neighbours and feared by foreigners.[26] His only drawback was his greed, which made him shelter the robbers.[27]

Suraj Mal's death embittered Jawahir Singh. He joined hands with the Sikhs with a view to continue his struggle against Najib-ud-duala. But he had to leave the territories of Haryana. By the instigation of the Raja of Jaipur, Jawahir Singh was assassinated in August 1768 in Agra Fort. His weak successors Ratan Singh and Nawal Singh could not maintain their position. Consequently, the Jat powers began to decline.

Najib-ud-duala was troubled not only by Suraj Mal and his successors, but by the turbulent peasantry of Haryana as well. Due to the prevailing anarchy and confusion the peasants of the adjoining villages of Sonepat revolted against the Delhi *Sarkar* and refused to pay the revenue,[28] usurped the land and cattle of others and started looting. Their leaders belonged to a body of Jats of village Buana[29] (16 miles north-west of Delhi). Najib-ud-duala sacked the villages and slaughtered the inhabitants. It is said that nearly two thousand men were slain and about the same number of women and children were carried away as prisoners.[30] Many villages were set on fire. Consequently, it created terror among the villagers and all the *Zamindars* submitted and paid the land revenue.[31]

Like the peasants of northern Haryana, Najib-ud-duala had to fight with the people of Rohtak and Hissar who refused to pay the land revenue. In October 1765, he attacked the villages of Kaluwas

(30 miles west of Rohtak) and set it on fire. The villagers sought safety in flight, but some of them were slain or made prisoners.[32] Najib-ud-duala also plundered the adjoining areas of Bhiwani, where the *Zamindars* had turned recalcitrant.

The Ascendancy of the Sikhs

With the eclipse of the Marathas in the Battle of Panipat in 1761 and the death of Suraj Mal in the end of 1763, Haryana became just a no man's land, and an easy prey to the rapacity of the Sikh *misldars*.

The Sikhs started their raids after Crossing the Sutlej. The raids of the Sikhs became an annual feature.[33] They conquered and occupied Sarhind and murdered Zaina Khan, the Afghan Governor of Sarhind, on 14th January 1764. They occupied northern Haryana which included Ambala, Karnal, Thanesar and Panipat.[34] Jassa Singh Ahluwalia occupied Naraingarh, Jai Singh Nishanwalia captured Kharar, Karam Singh Sahid occupied Shahjadpur and Kesari. Gajpat Singh of the house of Phul seized a large tract of country, including the districts of Jind and Safidon.[35] Ala Singh and Amar Singh of Patiala also occupied a part of Haryana. In 1767 Desu Singh founded a Sikh State at Kaithal. In 1777, by a treaty, Hansi, Hissar and Rohtak were restored to the Mughals and Fatehabad and Rania remained in the jurisdiction of Patiala.

In November 1764 when Jawahir Singh attacked Najib-ud-duala's territory the *Budha* Dal of Sikhs, under the leadership of Jassa Singh Ahluwalia, plundered upper Doab. In January 1765 they reached Buriaghat where a formal treaty was made between the Sikhs and the Jats. Jawahir Singh himself went to meet the Sikh leaders on an elephant, but he was not well received. Anyhow he made treaty and agreed to pay subsidy equivalent to the salary of 15,000 soldiers. Najib-ud-duala sent Hafiz Rahmat Khan with 6,000 troops but he had to retreat his steps after sometime.

In the meantime Najib-ud-duala had been alarmed by the activities of the Sikhs and sent Meghraj, as his emissary to Ahmad Shah Abdali. Abdali came to India and advanced towards Lahore. Paying no attention to Jawahir Singh, the Sikhs suddenly rushed back to the Punjab, and continued to harass the Abdali troops till their retreat in March 1765.

The Sikhs assembled at Amritsar in September 1765 and decided to plunder Haryana and the Doab. They divided themselves into two parts at Sarhind. The *Tarun Dal* entered into Saharanpur after Crossing at Buriaghat. The *Buddha Dal*, which consisted of about 25,000 horses and was led by Jassa Singh, Tara Singh and Sham Singh, raided the Haryana territory, and laid the people under contribution.[36] But Najib-ud-duala tackled them.

In 1766, the Sikhs attacked Najib-ud-duala in the districts of Sonepat and Panipat. This time they succeeded in reaching up to the outskirts of Delhi and got immense booty.

In December 1767, the Sikhs under the leadership of Jassa Singh again took possession of northern Haryana up to Karnal. They gave a crushing defeat to Najib-ud-duala and compelled him to vacate the capital. In fact, they could have assumed the role of the king-makers of Delhi, but they lost the opportunity due to the differences among their leaders.

In January 1770, the Sikhs again raided in the *paraganas* of Panipat and Karnal and plundered every village and even menaced Delhi.[37] Najib-ud-duala made the last effort to subdue them, but failed. However, the death of Najib-ud-duala on 31st October 1770 terminated the Afghan rule over the region.

In April-May 1772, the Sikhs defeated Mughal Ali Khan, the Governor designate of Sarhind. This frightened the Mughal Emperor Shah Alam II and the Maratha Chief, Jankoji who was posted at Delhi. Jankoji immediately moved towards Panipat and Karnal to oust the Sikhs. However, he reached Pehowa (16 miles from Thanesar) and after bathing there in the sacred tank, returned to the capital.[38] Perhaps his mission was to collect further information about the Sikh raids.

In January 1774, the Sikhs again appeared on the scene of Delhi. They attacked and looted Shahdara on the night of January 18, 1774. At that time the Gujars were also looting Shahdara. The Emperor tried to take the Sikhs into confidence. He invited 1,000 Sikhs for fighting the Gujars. But Abdul Ahmad Khan, the *faujdar* of Sarhind, torpedoed the move. He appointed Samru as his *Naib* but the Sikhs pestered him and compelled him to leave Haryana.

So it would be clear from the above account that with the disaster of Panipat, it was a complete anarchy and political confusion in Haryana. With the termination of the stable central government at Delhi, it had become the exploiting ground for the Sikhs. A number of petty principalities were established by the Sikhs.

Haryana under the Rohilla Chiefs

On 6th January 1772 Shah Alam, a puppet emperor was brought from Allahabad to Delhi with the help of Mahadji Sindhia (1727-1794).[39] In fact, the Sikhs, as told, had already lost the opportunity to be called as king-makers due to the lack of unity among their chiefs.[40] However, Mahadji also could not encash his support as there was a great confusion in the Maratha camp after the death of Peshwa Madho Rao. According to some historians the Maratha fortune declined not at Panipat but from the premature death of Madho Rao, one of the ablest of the Peshwas.[41]

Zabita Khan, the son of late Najib-ud-duala tried to consolidate his power in Delhi. Consequently, Shah Alam in league with his Maratha allies thought of teaching Zabita Khan a lesson. The Maratha attacked Pathergarh and snatched it from Zabita Khan after a siege. But there was quarrel on the division of the spoils. They offered only a part of it to the Emperor. Besides, the Marathas demanded the districts of Panipat, Saharanpur and Meerut. The Emperor only offered the territories of Anupshahr and Karnal. The above event created rift and tensions betwèen the Emperor and Mahadji Sindhia. Consequently Mahadji could not achieve the prime position at the Delhi Court.

On the contrary Mirza Najaf Khan, one of the Rohilla Sardars, had won the confidence of Shah Alam. He made a confederacy against the Maratha and ousted them from Delhi. Now Shah Alam was the nominal ruler and Najaf Khan, like Najib-ud-duala, was the real authority at Delhi till his death in 1782. In Haryana he was given *parganas* of Hansi and Hissar. After consolidating his power Mirza Najaf Khan resolved to occupy the neighbouring territories of Haryana. His army attacked Gurgaon, Rewari and Jhajjar. He also tried to give a lesson to Nawal Singh, the successor of Jawahir Singh of Bharatpur and seized the mud fort of Maidengarhi on 17th August 1773.[42] He also got early possession of Ballabhgarh due to the defeat of Ajit and Hira Singh. He himself encamped at Sikri-Fatehpur.

After humiliating the refractory chiefs of western Haryana, Najaf Khan sent his troops to conquer the remaining territories.

Most of the *Zamindars* submitted without any considerable resistance.[43] Shah Alam also proceeded to suppress the rebellion of *Zamindars* of Mahendergarh and Narnaul. After a short resistance they also surrendered.[44]

Now, Najaf Khan paid attention towards northern Haryana *i.e.* Karnal, Jind, Shahabad, Thanesar and Ambala which were still under the Sikh Chiefs.

In the winter of 1774, the Sikhs under the leadership of Amar Singh of Patiala marched against the Bhatti chief. They captured the fort of Begran in Hissar District.[45] They also took possession of Fathehabad and Sirsa and invested Rania (8 miles west of Sirsa) which was under the control of Muhammad Amin Khan Bhatti.[46]

Meanwhile, Shah Alam sent Rahim Dad Khan, the Gover nor of Hansi, to attack Raja Gajpat Singh of Jind, but the former was defeated. Gajpat Singh took possession of parts of Gohana and Rohtak.[47] But soon Najaf Khan recovered Karnal and parts of Rohtak from the Sikhs.[48] A conciliatory meeting was also arranged at Jind in which a compromise was made. Amar Singh surrendered the districts of Hansi, Hissar and parts of Rohtak and was allowed to retain Fathehabad, Rania and Sirsa.[49] Gajpat Singh of Jind was also allowed to retain seven villages from the territory he had seized.[50]

Anyhow, during the above period, Sikhs extended their influence and territory upto Delhi and Zabita Khan made cordial relations with them. Perhaps the latter also embraced the religion of the Sikhs, adopted their dress, and changed his name to Dharm Singh.[52] Mirza Najaf Khan sent Abdul Qasim Khan but he was defeated in the battle of Aminnagar on llth March, 1776.

Next year, Mirza Najaf Khan himself led the campaign with a force of 5,000 soldiers and a strong artillery.[53] He reached upto the plains of Panipat. Zabita Khan requested for a treaty which was readily accepted. Zabita Khan gave his sister in marriage to Najaf Khan and his daughter to the son of the latter.[54] In return Zabita Khan's territory was restored. Najaf Khan now appointed Ahmad Dad, as Governor of Sarhind. So in this way, the northern Haryana also came under the administrative control of the Najaf Khan.

But in 1778, Mirza Najaf Khan had to face the Sikh rebellion in the north. The Sikhs defeated Ahmad Dad, the Governor of Sarhind and compelled him to retreat from Sarhind,[55] The Emperor

Shah Alam deputed Abdul Ahmad Khan to suppress the revolt. But he was interested in secretly establishing his own authority in the northern Haryana. So Abdul Ahmad Khan appointed Sayyaid Khan his son-in-law, as *Faujdar* of Sonepat-Panipat districts on February 5, 1778.[56]

On June 3, 1779, Abdul Ahmad Khan, marched towards Karnal with a army of 20,000 troops. On the way, all the *Zamindars* or the chiefs who resisted were subdued and charged. At Karnal, Gopal Singh, a *Zamindar* cordially received the Prince and the General, but the former was asked to pay a tribute of two lakhs. The Sikḥ chiefs were also asked to pay the annual tributes. Bhai Dehsu Singh, the Chief of Kaithal also came to meet at a Karnal. But it is said that on the advice of Gajpat Singh, all the Sikh leaders, who had come to pay respect to the Prince, were arrested. This alarmed the other Sikh chiefs.

Abdul Ahmad Khan demanded three lakhs of rupees from Dehsu Singh on a charge of not having paid his arrears of revenue.[57] Dehsu Singh hesitated but eventually agreed to pay 2½ lakhs as the tribute, and for the payment of the balance, he gave his son Lal Singh as a hostage.[58]

On 13th September 1779, Amar Singh of Patiala also sent his Diwan Nanun Mal with a tribute of five lakhs of rupees on the condition that the Imperial Army should immediately retreat from Karnal. Amar Singh also presented a *nazarana* of ₹ 25,000 to the Prince. Rut Abdul Ahmad did not pay any heed and marched towards the territory of Patiala. He crossed the river Saraswati near Pehowa on 23rd September 1779 and reached Kuhram (15 miles southeast of Patiala) on 28th September 1779. A battle was fought on October 7, 1779 in which Abdul Ahmad came out victorious. Meanwhile Amar Singh secretly got assistance from the Sikh chiefs like the Kanhiya Sardars Jai Singh and Hakikat Singh, Jassa Singh Ramgharia, Tara Singh Ghaba, Jodh Singh of Wazirabad, Phulkia chiefs of Jind, Nabha, Bhadur and Malod.[59] On 14th October 1779 Amar Singh compelled Abdul Ahmad Khan to retreat. It is said that Amar Singh followed him up to Panipat. Abdul Ahmad Khan returned to Delhi on 5th November 1779.[60] Later Amar Singh died in 1781 of dropsy brought on by excessive drinking leaving a minor son.[61] Due to the great famine of 1783 in Sirsa and other parts, the Sikhs, could not recover the territory.[62]

As the Emperor heard the news of the defeat of Abdul Ahmad Khan on 16th October 1779, he informed Mirza Najaf Khan who was not there. Najab Khan reached Delhi on 12th November 1779. But the Emperor, with the ill-advice of Abdul Ahmad Khan, had now changed his mind and did not allow Najaf Khan to enter into the capital. It enraged Mirza Najaf Khan who after a few skirmishes arrested Abdul Ahmad Khan. Later the Emperor invited Najaf Khan who was appointed as Regent Plenipotentiary (*Vakil-i-Mutlaq*) on 16th November 1779. Now Najaf Khan sent Mirza Shafi against the Sikhs in the Sonepat-Panipat Districts,[63] who wrested the territory from the Sikhs.

During this period, Balwant Singh the Raja of Mahendergarh had occupied many villages in the Hansi-Hissar districts, which belonged to Najif Quli's *jagir*. Consequently, Najaf proceeded to Mahendergarh in the last week of November. As he found the water scarce, he adopted foul methods. He invited the Raja for negotiating a treaty but treacherously assassinated his son alongwith 30 other Rajput nobles on 4th December 1779. In the meanwhile Najaf made enough arrangement for water supply and beseiged the fort. On the other side Begum Samru alongwith her force had joined the besiegers. On 5th February 1780 Narnaul was plundered by the Mughals.[64] Similarly on 14th February 1780 Mitrasen Ahir, the Raja of Rewari, had to surrender.

Maratha Supremacy over Haryana

With the death of Mirza Najaf Khan on 6th April 1782 a period of uncertainty, anarchy and confusion prevailed. The Sikhs, the Mewatis and the Gujars started plundering northern Haryana and the adjacent territories of Delhi. In the Mughal court also the game of dirty politics and intrigues started. Mahadji received the invitation from Afrasiyab Khan, the Mughal noble and the former met the old Emperor on 22nd October 1784.[65] But Afrasiyab Khan was soon murdered on 22nd November by Zain-ul-abudha, the brother of late Mirza Shafi Khan, and the latter fled to Mahadji and sought refuge.[66] Very soon Mahadji had become the supreme authority at Delhi.[67] The Emperor bestowed upon him the administration of the *subas* of Delhi and Agra.[68] Mahadji asked Ambaji Ingle to supervise the administration of Delhi. The latter was appointed as the *faujdar* of Sonepat.

Ambaji Ingle, first of all, paid attention towards the increasing trouble by the Gujars in Delhi and its environs. He subdued them through ruthless methods. Many Gujars were arrested near Surajpur and nearly 200 of them were put to the sword.[69] Several raids were made on their villages. Ambaji continued his campaigns and succeeded in establishing peace and order.[70]

Thereafter, Ambaji moved towards Panipat to subdue the Sikh freebooters. At Bakhtawar (13 miles north of Delhi) a group of nine Sikh chiefs of the Panipat territory met him to Mardi 27, 1785. Mahadji concluded a treaty on May 10, 1785 in which Mahadji accepted the political supremacy of the Sikhs in the Punjab[71] while the latter promised to refrain from raiding the adjoining territories of Delhi.[72] But the treaty remained short.

In 1786 the Sikhs again commenced their plundering raids. Mahadji made serious efforts to handle the Sikh affairs tactfully. He feared that the Sikhs might join hands with Gulam Qadir, the son of Zabita Khan.

In 1787, Ambaji moved towards Punjab. Now some Sikh sardars including Bhagat Singh helped him with one thousand troops. Ambaji also tried to get help of Karam Singh of Shahabad and Gurdit Singh of Ambala, and promised six annas a day per *sawar*. But in return they demanded a large portion of *jagirs* as it had been bestowed on Bhagat Singh. Anyhow, Ambaji could not make much headway in the Punjab. On his return journey he was accompanied by Bhagat Singh and six other sardars who had joined him at Panipat one of them Rao Singh, having gone away with Ghulam Qadir.

Now the political climate of the country suddenly changed. The sudden rise of Ghulam Qadir, the grandson of Najib-ud-duala and the son of Zabita Khan, had proved that despite the death of Rohilla chief, the anti-Maratha party was still left with a formidable leader.[73] Ghulam Qadir was a very ambitious, crude, cruel and greedy person. Encouraged by the defeat of Mahadji at Jaipur, and instigated by his ambition of plundering treasury,[74] Ghulam Qadir ruslied towards Delhi, sought assistance of the rebellious and disgruntled elements and reached there on 24th August 1787. He deposed and blinded the old Emperor, plundered the Imperial Palace and the city in search of imaginary treasures, placed Mirza Bedar Bakht, son of Ahmad Shah on the throne and dishonoured and disgraced the royal family.[75] The old Emperor sent message to Mahadji for his earliest arrival. Mahadji reached Rewari after September 2, 1787.

Before regaining Delhi and fighting with Ghulam Qadir, Mahadji decided to win over Mirza Ismail Beg,[76] the nephew and successor of Muhmmad Beg Hamadani, in October 1788 and bestowed upon him the *jagir* of the Rewari-Narnaul area.[77] In fact the above State was previously given to Najaf Quli Khan, the adopted son of late Mirza Najaf Khan. It was a diplomatic move so that both the Mirzas might fight for the same *jagir*.[78]

However, Ghulam Qadir became cautious and withdrew from Delhi as he heard the news of Mahadji, carrying with him several of the Princes of the Emperor with a view to a future compromise with the Emperor or to creating a controversy between him and Mahadji. The former was arrested on 8th December. Mahadji tried to induce Ghulam Qadir to reveal the hiding-places of his Delhi loot, but in vain. The old Emperor wrote a letter to Mahadji telling him that if he did not extract Ghulam Qadir's eyes, the Emperor would abdicate the throne and retire to Mecca in a beggar's grab. Consequently, Ghulam Qadir's eyes were dug out[81] and sent in a casket to Shah Alam. Ghulam Qadir was put to the sword on 3rd March 1789.[82]

The murder of Ghulam Qadir was a great relief to the Mughal ruler, Shah Alam who heartily welcomed Mahadji and described him as 'his dear son'. In fact, now Mahadji had become the supreme administrator of Delhi.[83] Perhaps he was the only living Maratha who knew the problems of northern India fully due to his experience.

Now Mahadji turned his eyes towards Haryana. It was divided into a number of small principalities. Three main powers may be mentioned. The northern Haryana including Ambala, Karnal and Jind had been under the Sikh chiefs. Najaf Quli Khan had occupied the territories of Rewari, Narnaul, Gurgaon, Jhajjar and Rohtak. He posed to be an independent ruler, with Gokalgarh (2 miles from Rewari) as his capital. The north-east territory of Haryana was under the Bhattis. They had in their possession Fatehabad, Rania and Sirsa. So practically the whole of Haryana was independent. Mahadji had to make tremendous efforts to conquer and administer the territories.[84]

In 1789, Ambaji Ingle marched towards northern Haryana to beat the Sikh raiders. Having failed in his efforts, Mahadji tried to make a treaty with the Sikhs with the help of Beghal Singh. In fact, it may be called a diplomatic pact on the part of Mahadji.

Like Ambaji Ingle, Mahadji sent Ismail Beg against Najaf Quli Khan, who had in his possession the territories of Gurgaon, Rewari, Narnaul and Kanud.[86] Ismail Beg occupied Gurgoan, Beri (in Rohtak district) and Rewari. He gave the administration of this area to his father Munim Beg.[87] Najaf Quli Khan fought bravely against Ismail Beg from Kanud but he could not resist for long. He fled and kept himself in the fort of Kanud. Ismail Beg got immense booty. He also sent his army to capture Narnaul, Rohtak and Dadri which were occupied.[88]

In the end of 1789 the Sikhs had spread over not only in the whole of the Punjab and Haryana but also made incursions up to the frontier of Oudh territory. In the autumn of 1790, ten thousand Sikhs raided the frontier of Oudh and captured Lieutenant-Colonel Robert Stuart, the Commander of the English battalion.[89] Perhaps it was to distress the Marathas and to plunder the Oudh territory.[90] Robert Stuart was confined in the fort of Thanesar belonging to Bhanga Singh. Later in 1791, the former was released through the efforts of Begum Samru.[91]

In the meanwhile, Mahadji sent Tukoji Holkar to secure Mewat against the Sikh raids. Gopal Hari, the *thanedar* of Nuh (25 miles south of Gurgaon), a Holkar's man, attempted to seize the adjoining *mahal* of Nimaksar. Mirza Ismail Beg got irritated. His men killed Gopal Hari. Ismail Beg also protested to Mahadji in the following words:

> "if you want to dismiss me say so, and I shall go elsewhere for service. If you want to fight with me com on. But do not set other people against me."[92]

Anyhow, this embittered Ismail Beg and created doubts about Maratha good faith. Consequently, Ismail Beg made alliance with the Rajputs—the Rajas of Jodhpur and Jaipur—against the Marathas in February 1790. The Rajput Rajas promised to pay him twelve lakhs, out of which two lakhs were given as advance, and remaining ten lakhs were to be paid after the commencement of war with Mahadji.[93] In return the family of Ismail had to be kept in Jaipur.[94]

Mahadji sent his troops under the supervision of Gopal Bhau assisted by Jiva Dada Bakshi and Colonel De Boigne, who marched toward Rewari.[95] Later Ambaji Ingle met the former at Alwar. Holkar and Ali Bahadur had also sent their troops numbering 4,000 and 1,000 respectively. Mahadji also acquired the help of a body of 2,000 cavalry of Najaf Quli Khan, as the latter was restored in the *jagirs* lately usurped by Ismail Beg. The ruler of Machiri also helped him.

The expedition commenced in May 1790. Gopal Bhau besieged and occupied the fort of Gokalgarh on 16th July 1791 and kept Ismail Beg's father Munim Beg as a prisoner in chains in Agra Fort.[96] Disgusted with the Rajput rulers Ismail Beg moved toward Kanud, as the widow of Najaf Quli Khan (who had died on 23rd August 1791) offered the Kanud fort to him and she also offered to marry him. It took Ismail Beg two months to decide his future planning. By this time the widow had changed her mind due to the changed political circumstances. She now resolved to fight with Ismail Beg. She with her captains Madari Khan Mewati, Gulab Singh and others, put up her adopted son Ismail Khan as ruler of Kanud. She did not allow the troops of Ismail Beg to enter the fort of Kanud. Consequently he had to run away towards the hills of Madhogarh and set up a post near it.

Khande Rao now marched towards Madhogarh and occupied it on 16th February 1792. Ismail Beg attacked the fort of Kanud when the widow of Najaf Quli Khan died. The troops capitulated to the Maratha forces on 15th April, 1792. The Maratha's success was complete and decisive. Ismail Beg was captured, imprisoned in the Agra fort and put to death in March 1794.[97] In the meanwhile, Mahadji also ousted the Bhattis and occupied Fathehabad, Rania and Sirsa.

After conquering all the above territories Mahadji divided Haryana region into four districts as under:[98]

1. Delhi—it included the Emperor's palace and family and the surrounding area of Haryana.
2. Panipat—it constituted the present districts of Karnal, Sonepat, Ambala and Kurukshetra.
3. Hissar—it included Hissar and some part of the present Rohtak district.
4. Mewat—it included Gurgaon, Rewari, Narnaul and Mahendergarh.

Now Mahadji made some efforts to have cordial relations with the Sikhs. But he could not succeed in the effort. After Mahadji Sindhia's death at Poona on 12th Feb., 1794, his northern viceroy

Gopal Bhau appointed Devji Gaula and Bapu Malhar at Panipat, and Apa Khande Rao who was in charge of the Delhi district at Jhajjar.[99] In November 1794, Daulat Rao Sindhia appointed Lakhwa Dada his viceroy of the North in place of Gopal Bhau. Later Lakhwa Dada appointed his deputy Nana Rao at Karnal and allowed him to collect the revenue from the *cis*-Sutlej country. But the Sikhs chiefs refused to pay. The Patiala queen and Bhanga Singh of Thanesar defeated Nana Rao and compelled him to retire to Delhi in October 1795.[100]

First European Adventurer in Haryana

Like the indigenous invaders, raiders and adventurers Haryana also became the victim of the foreign intruders. The career of George Thomas the first successful foreign adventurer is marked by 'the brilliancy and briefness of a meteor.'[101]

Born in poor Irish family of Tipperary about 1756;[102] became an ordinary sailor; arrived on a British ship at Madras in 1781/82; was appointed as gunner in Nizam's army; reached Delhi on foot in 1787; and received commission in the European corps of Begum Samru (formerly known as Zebun-Nissa),[103] the Queen of Sardhana near Meerut. It is said that George Thomas's personality attracted Begum and she married to him one of her adopted daughters'child from some European officer in her corps. Later George Thomas was appointed as collector of the sub-division of Tappal (32 miles of northwest of Aligarh) in Begum's *jagir*. He collected the revenue and gradually doubled the proceeds, subdued the law-breakers, and scared away Sikh raiders.[104] But soon his relation with Begum Samru got strained. Perhaps he became the victim of the intrigues of Le Vasseau, the leader of the French Party at her court, who later became the husband of the Begum. George Thomas was dismissed. But George Thomas resisted and this resulted into his arrest and confinement in September 1791. Anyhow, he was released by the assistance of Shah Nizamuddin, an agent of Mahadji at the Delhi Court. He reached Anupshahr and remained there as captain for about two years in the private corps of mercenaries.

In October 1793, George Thomas was invited by the Maratha General Apa Khande Rao who directed him to raise a battalion of 1,000 regular infantry and 100 cavalry.[105] George served under him for four years.

In 1794 Apa Khande Rao enlarged his troops and George Thomas was assigned the territories of Tijara, Tapukra and Firozepur Jhirka as fiefs for the maintenance of the army.[106] But before he could obtain his fiefs, he had to prove himself equal to the occasion. In March-July 1794, he occupied Tijara, looted Bahadurgarh (in Rohtak district) and captured Jhajjar and marched towards Pataudi. All these territories were included in his *jagir*.[107] Here he built a fort known as Georgegarh which came to be popularly known as Jahazgarh. He also subdued Bakht, the rebel *zamindar* of Rewari. He also compelled Ganga Bishan, an Ahir, who was one of the strongest *zamindars* of Haryana having 14,000 fighting men on his side.[108] He also captured Beri.[109]

When George Thomas was busy in suppressing the refractory villages, Begum Samru also moved against him from her capital—Sardhana. Perhaps she was instigated by Le Vasseau to attack George. Consequently she encamped about 34 miles south-east of Jhajjar.[110] Her army was comparatively numerous. It consisted of 4 battalions of infantry, 20 companies of artillery and about 400 cavalry, while on George Thomas's sides were only 2,000 men, 10 pieces of artillery, 500 irregulars and 200 cavalry.[111] However, Begum Samru could not succeed in her game as there was revolt in her own camp due to Personal rivalries and intrigues between the Chief-Commander Le Vasseau and a German Legois, the latter being a friend of George Thomas. In this internal conflict, Le Vasseau committed suicide and Begum Samru was wounded. However, the serious danger was averted very soon.[112] Now George Thomas moved towards Narnual and occupied it. Apa Khande Rao bestowed on him an elephant, a palanquin shawls and some pieces of artillery.[113]

In 1795, about 5,000 Sikh raiders under Karam Singh made intrusion in the Maratha district in Doab. Apa Khande Rao sent George Thomas towards Saharanpur. George maintained peace and order in the area and the Sikh-freebooters fled away. Now Lakhwa Dada appointed Thomas as Warden of the marches of guard the Yamuna frontier of the upper Doab, and his contingent were raised to 2,000 infantry, 200 cavalry and 16 pieces of artillery. The *paraganas* of Panipat, Sonepat and Karnal were given to him for his maintenance.

During the next year, George Thomas remained busy in fighting the Sikhs who continued to create trouble throughout the year on both banks of the Yamuna.

On 25th June, 1797, Apa Khande Rao was drowned in the river Yamuna. He was succeeded by Vaman Rao.[115] At this time, the Maratha administration was fast deteriorating. George Thomas could not get the due money from the Marathas for the maintenance of the troops. Being disgusted with the indifferent attitude of his Maratha employers, he had started plundering. Encamping at Jhajjar, he raided Urika (35 miles northeast of Jhunjhunnu in Rajasthan) and took a ransom of ₹ 52,000 from it.[116] In reality now George Thomas adopted the career of a private robber captain for his living.[117] In the battle of Fatehpur (30 miles north of Sikri) in Jaipur kingdom in which he joined Vaman Rao and took possession of the city in February 1798, he was perturbed with the role of the Maratha cavalry.[118]

Now George Thomas established an independent kingdom with its capital at Hansi. His kingdom was situated in the west of the Rewari-Delhi-Karnal districts and south of Patiala.

Harbert Compton writes about the area:

> "To the north-west of Jhajjar lay a tract of territory known as Haryana or the Greenland. . . . Haryana at the end of the last century was a veritable no man's land, acknowledging no master, and tempting none. In turn the prey of many succeeding invaders, it had for many years been a recognised battle-field for contending powers."[119]

Sir Jadunath Sarkar describes this tract in the following words:

> "Oval in shape, with ill-defined and ever-shifting frontiers, it extended 32 to 48 miles in different directions. On the north lay the Ghaggar river which separates it from the lands under Sikh occupation; the west the country of the predatory Bhatti tribe, beyond which lay the deserts of Bikaner. The south was bounded by the Rewari district."[120]

George Thomas made efforts to provide his subjects with the basic needs of life. As there was scarcity of water, he constructed Wells. He eacouraged people to live there. its population rose to 6,000. He established a mint and coined his own rupee known as Sikka-i-Sahib. In his own words, "I established a mint, and coined my own rupee which of made current in my army and country;

cast my own artiliery, coramenced making muskets, matchlocks and powder."[121] Now he had a force of eight regiment of foot, a thousand horsemen and about fifty guns.[122] According to Sarkar the revenue yielded by the 14 *paraganas*[123] consisting of 253 villages was ₹ 2,86,000 and of the five *paraganas* which were held by the Marathas containing 151 villages was 1,44,000 in 1798.

Now George Thomas, the Irish Rajah, conquered the fort of Gokalgarh in September 1798, which was under the possession of a local governor of Mahadji. Then he marched against Bhag Singh, the Rajah of Jind. But Bhag Singh was assisted by the Sikh chiefs like the Kaithal commanders Sawan Singh, Saman Singh and Diwan Ramdyal; Gurdit Singh of Ladwa; Bhanga Singh and Mehtab Singh of Thanesar.[124] So George Thomas was forced to retreat at the end of February 1799. In a peace treaty the *status quo* was restored.[125]

In January 1800, George Thomas made an attack on Patiala at the request of princess Sahib Kaur, who had been imprisoned by her brother, Sahib Singh, the Raja of Patiala. George plundered the city and made a treaty in March 1800 with the Raja of Patiala. It was agreed that the districts of Budsikri, Jamalpur and Toham from Patiala, Kanpori from Kaithal and Safidon from Jind would be given to George Thomas.

Then George Thomas besieged Sirsa, a fort belonging to the tribe of Muslim Bhatti. He remained there for seven months and collected huge booty and captured Bhatner.[126]

In January 1801, George Thomas again attacked Patiala to support the princess Sahib Kaur. In the beginning he achieved marginal success but later the united Khalsa forces repulsed him.[127] It became difficult to him to retreat easily and safely.

Again in the middle of April-May 1801, George Thomas moved towards Jind. He invaded Kaithal. But now, Bhag Singh of Jind had got the support of General Perron, whom Daulat Rao Sindhia had made the supreme commander in North India. Several attempts for mutual friendship were made, but all in vain. In September 1801, Perron sent Major Louis Bourguien with ten battalions of sepoys, 3,000 cavalry and 500 Rohilla Ali Ghol to attack Thomas, who was then plundering Jind. George Thomas retreated. Another force of Perron under L.F. Smith and E. Falix Smith attacked Georgegarh. Both the Smiths were defeated. They joined Major Bourguien who was marching towards Georgegarh.

On Ist October, 1801 a severe battle took place in which about 600 casualties on each side took place.[128] But in the meantime, Sikhs came to help Bourguien. They cut the supply line of George Thomas and the scarcity of food-stuff prevailed in his camp. Flour began to sell at eight seers for a rupee. George Thomas fought bravely but had to eventually seek safety in flight. He left the fort on the night of 10th November 1801 with a small cavalry. Georgegarh was captured. Major Bourguien followed George Thomas to Hansi. By this time George Thomas was without men, money or ammunition. At last when he was surrounded,[129] he surrendered to Bourguien on 23rd December 1801 and opened the gates of the capital. He was allowed to go to British India. He reached Anupshahr in January 1802. He arrived in Berhampur in Bengal where he died on 22nd August 1802. He was buried there.[130] The Georgegarh fort later came into the possession of the Nawab of Jhajjar and he named it Hassangarh.[131]

However, Haryana remained under the control ofthe Maratha till 1803 A.D. On 11th September 1803 the Anglo-Maratha war broke out. General Lake marched towards Delhi and overthrew the Marathas and disperssed the Sikhs.[132] The latter soon showed their allegiance and Bhai Lal Singh of Kaithal, Bhag Singh of Jind and later Bhanga Singh of Thanesar helped the British.[133] With the battle of Laswari on Ist Nov. 1803 the Maratha power vanished from northern India.

On December 30, 1803 Daulat Rao Sindhia ceded the territory of Haryana to the British East India Company through the treaty of Surji Anjangaon. Haryana was included in the Presidency of Bengal with a resident at Delhi to administer it. The British kept under their direct supervision the territories which generally included Panipat, Sonepat, Samalka, Ganur, Haveli Palam, Nuh, Hatheen, Tijara Bhora, Tapukara, Sohna, Rewari, Indri-Palwal etc. These territories were placed under the administration of the Resident as "assigned territory."[134] The remaining region was divided among different chiefs and sardars. For example, Nawab Isa Khan and Ahmad Baksh Khan were granted their old *jagirs*. Faiz Talab Khan and Ahmad Baksh Khan were given the *paraganas* of Pataudi and Loharu, Firozpur-Jhirka respectively. Rao Tej Singh got the territory of 87 villages in Rewari *paragana*. Similarly, Murtaza Khan and Muhammad Ali Khan got Hodal and Palwal *paraganas* respectively. Rohtak, Meham, Beri, Hissar,

Hansi, Agroha, Tosham Barwala, and Jamalpur were given to Rohilla chief Bambu Khan. Later they were transferred to Abdus Samad Khan. Muhammad Ali Khan of Muzaffarnagar got possession of some villages in Karnal. Begum Samru of Sardhana also got some villages in *paraganas* of Karnal and Gurgaon.[135] Other *jagirs* remained as earlier. For example, Nawab Dilar Khan of Kunjpura, Raja Bhanga Singh of Thanesar, Bhai Lal Singh of Kaithal, Gurdit Singh of Ladwa and the Sardar of Shamgarh remained in possession of their territories.

In fact the treaty of Surji Anjangaon marks "the tragic end of the Mughal empire as a political institution,"[136] it also marked the end of the period of great anarchy in Haryana and proclaimed the emergence of the British rule in this region. The whole period from 1761 to 1803 may be compared to a drama of five acts in which the Jats, the Sikhs, the Rohillas, the Marathas and the European adventurers played the dominating role. It ends with the recession of all these petty powers and the emergence of a new one—the East India Company.

NOTES

1. G. S. Sardesai: *The Main Carrents of Maratha Histoty,* (Bombay, 1933), p. 148.
2. *See* R.C. Majumdar: *The Maratha Supremacy* (Bombay, 1977).
3. W. Francklin: *The History of the Reign of Shah Alam* (Allahabad, 1915), p. 17.
4. Ganda Singh: *Ahmad Shah Durrani,* p. 288; H.R. Gupta; *Studies in Later Mughal History of the Punjab,* p. 186.
5. For the Flistory of Rohillas and Najib-ud-duala please see George Forester; *A Journey from Bengal to England,* (London, 1798), Vol. I, pp. 115-149.
6. Jagdish Narain Sarkar: *A Study of Eighteenth Century India,* (Calcutta, 1976), Vol. I, p. 380.
7. *Ibid.,* pp. 380-81.
8. *Ibid.,* p. 381.
9. *Ibid.,* pp. 385; K.R. Qanungo: *Historical Essays,* (Agra, 1960), pp. 42-48.
10. Jagdish Narain Sarkar: *op. cit.,* p. 385.
11. J.N. Sarkar: *Fall of the Mughal Empire,* Vol. II, (Calcutta, 1971), p. 180.
12. For detail see Jagdish Narain Sarkar; *op. cit.,* pp. 385-390.
13. K.R. Qanungo, *op. cit.,* p. 46.
14. J. Allan, W. Haig and H.H. Dodwell: *The Cambridge Shorter History of India,* (New York, 1934), p. 472.
15. *Ibid.,* p. 472.
16. *Ibid.,* p. 473.
17. *Ibid.*
18. S.R. Sharma; *The Crescent in India,* (Bombay, 1934), p. 755.
19. *Ibid.,* p. 756.

20. Buddha Prakash: Haryana *Through the Ages,* (Kurukshetra, n.d.), p. 77.
21. C.A. Kincaid: *A History of the Maratha People,* (London, 1931), p. 337; H.R. Gupta: The Jat-Maratha Relations (1740-1760), *Haryana Studies in History and Culture,* (Kurukshetra, 1968, ed. Dr. K.C. Yadav), p. 71.
22. V.A. Smith: *The Oxford History of India,* (Oxford, 1923), p. 461.
23. Jagdish Narain Sarkar: *op. cit.,* p. 389.
24. H.G. Keen: *The Fall of the Mughal Empire,* (Delhi, 1971), p. 83.
25. J.N. Sarkar: Najib-ud-duala as the Dictator of Delhi, *Islamic Culture,* Vol. VII, (Hyderabad, 1934), p. 625; Grant Duff: *History of the Marathas,* p. 438.
26. Father Francois Xavier Wendal: *Accounts of the Jais* (in French), Quoted by J.N. Sarkar, *op. cit.,* Vol. II, 390.
27. *Ibid.,* p. 390.
28. *Ibid.,* p. 282.
29. *Ibid.*
30. *Ibid.,* p. 283.
31. *Ibid.*
32. *Ibid.,* p. 284.
33. *Ibid.,* p. 257.
34. *Karnal District Gazetteer* (Lahore, 1918), p. 21.
35. L.H. Griffin: *The Rajas of the Punjab,* (Lahore, 1870), p. 312.
36. J.N. Sarkar: *op. cit.,* Vol. II, p. 286.
37. A.C. Banerjee: *Peshwa Madho Rao I,* p. 132; J.N. Sarkar: *op. cit.,* Vol. II, p. 290.
38. L.H. Griffin: *The Rajas of Punjab,* p. 38.
39. Select Committee Letter dated 23rd January, 1772, *Fort William—Indian House Correspondence,* 1770-72, Vol. VI, (Ed. Bisheshwar Parshad, Delhi, 1960), p. 357; *see also* Dr. Prabha Chopra: *Delhi History and Places of Interest* (Delhi, 1970), p. 48. According to Francklin and Keen, Shah Alam returned to the capital on 25th December 1771. See Francklin *History of the Shah Alam* (Allahabad, 1915), p. 17; H.G. Keen: *op. cit.,* (Delhi, 1971), p. 98.
40. *Calendar of Persian Correspondence,* Vol. IV, p. 849.
41. G.S. Sardesai; *op. cit.,* p. 147; Grant Duff: *op. cit.,* Vol. II, p. 349.
42. J.N. Sarkar: *op. cit.,* Vol, III, p. 66.
43. Francklin: *op. cit.,* p. 38.
44. *Ibid.,* p. 83.
45. L.H. Griffin: *The Rajas of the Punjab,* p. 42.
46. *Ibid.*
47. *Ibid.,* p. 43.
48. *Ibid.*
49. *Ibid.,* p. 44.
50. *Ibid.,* p. 45.
51. J.D. Cunningham: *History of the Sikhs,* p. 105.
52. *Ibid.,* p. 105; Forester: *Travels,* Vol. I, p. 325: *see also* Browne: *Indian Tracts,* II, p. 29; Francklin: *op. cit.,* p. 72; *see* Article of Birender Verma: Sikh Challenge to Contemporary Powers in Northern India (1773-1799), *Punjab History Conference,* Proceedings, (26-27 April, 1975), p. 68.
53. H.G. Keen: *op. cit.* p. 126.

54. *Ibid.*
55. *Ibid.*
56. *Ibid.*, p. 128.
57. According to L.H. Griffin a demand of 4 lakhs rupees was made from Dehsu Singh, later the latter had agreed to pay ₹ 3 lakhs. See *The Rajas of the Punjab*, p. 5.
58. J.N. Sarkar: *op. cit.*, Vol. III, p. 123.
59. L.H. Griffin: *The Rajas of the Punjab*, p. 52.
60. J.N. Sarkar: *op. cit.*, Vol. III, p. 125.
61. L.H. Griffin: *The Rajas of the Punjab*, p. 53.
62. J.D. Cunningham: *op. cit.*, p. 105; L.H. Griffin: *op. cit.*, p. 57.
63. J.N. Sarkar: *op. cit.*, Vol. III, p. 130.
64. *Ibid.*, p. 140.
65. Grant Duff: *op. cit.*, p. 571.
66. R.C. Majumdar: *The Maratha Supremacy*, p. 389.
67. J.N. Sarkar: *op. cit*, Vol. III, p. 161; Dr. Prabha Chopra: *op. cit.*, p. 50.
68. Grant Duff: *op. cit.*, p. 572.
69. Prabha Chopra: *op. cit.*, p. 50.
70. J.N. Sarkar: *op. cit*. Vol. III, p. 210.
71. *Calendar of Persian Correspondent*, Vol. VI, No. 243.
72. *Ibid.*
73. J.N. Sarkar: *op. cit.*, Vol. IV, p. 1.
74. Letter to the Secret Committee of the Court of Directors, 6th Nov. 1788, *Fort-William—Indian House Correspondence*, Vol. XVI, p. 195; *See also* Letter to the Secret Committee dated 14 December, 1787, p. 164.
75. Latter to the Secret Committee of the Court of Directors, 6th November, 1788, *Fort William—Indian House Correspondence*, Vol. XIX, p. 195; See also Secret Letter to the Governor-Genera-in Council at Fort-William, dt. 15th April 1789, p. 39; *Poona Residency Correspondence* (Ed. J.N. Sarkar in English) Vol. I, pp. 154-55; J.N. Sarkar: *op. cit.*, Vol. III, pp. 308-10; H.G. Keen: *op, cit.*, p. 190; Sir W. Haig: *The Cambridge History of India*, Vol. IV, (Delhi, 1957J, p. 448; R.C. Majumdar: *The Maratha Supremacy*, p. 398: L.H. Griffin: *The Rajas of the Punjab*, p. 63; J.D. Cunningham : *op. cit.*, p. 109; Dr. Prabha Chopra : *op. cit.*, p. 51.
76. Letter to the Court of Directors, *Fort-William—Indian House Correspondence*, Vol. XVI, p. 172, Dated 15th December, 1787.
77. J.N. Sarkar: *op. cit.*, Vol. IV, p. 2.
78. *Ibid.*, pp. 7-8.
79. Letter to the Secret Committee of the Court of Directors, dated 6th November, 1788, *Fort-Willian— Indian House Correspondence*, Vol. XVI, p. 196.
80. J.N. Sarkar: *op. cit.*, Vol. IV, p. 8.
81. *Ibid.*, Vol. IV, p. 9.
82. *Ibid*. Vol III, p. 273; Grant Duff: *op. cit.*, Vol. III, Letter to the Secret Committee, 10th August, 1789, *Fort-Willian—Indian House Correspondence*, Vol. XVI, p. 246, XXVII; Elliot and Downson: *Ibratnama*, Vol. VIII, p. 254; Prabha Chopra: *op. cit.*, p. 51.

83. Grant Duff: *op. cit.,* Vol. III, pp. 207-208; *Fort-William—Indian House Correspondence,* Vol. XVI, p. XXXVI.
84. J.N. Sarkar: *op. cit.*, Vol. VI. p. 6.
85. *Hissar District Gazetteer*, p. 27.
86. It is now called Mahendergarh.
87. J.N. Sarkar: *op. cit.*, Vol. IV, p. 14.
88. *Ibid.*, p. 15.
89. Letter to the Court of Directors, 31st January, 1791: *Fort-William—Indian House Correspondence,* Vol. XVI, p. 363.
90. Letter to the Court of Directors, 12th March, 1791, *Ibid.*, Vol. XVI, p. 380.
91. Letter to the Court of Directors, 1st December, 1791, *Ibid,* Vol. XVI, p. 429.
92. J.N. Sarkar: *op. cit.*, Vol. IV, p. 17 (*see* footnote).
93. *Ibid.*
94. *Ibid.*
95. *Ibid.*, pp. 20.
96. *Ibid.*, p. 42, 47.
97. *Ibid.*, p. 46; Michael, Edward: *King of the World: The Life and Times of Shah Alam, Emperor of Hindustan,* (London, 1970), pp. 227-28; *Calendar of Persian Correspondence,* Vol. II, No. 153, (NAI Delhi, 1940-59).
98. R.C. Majumdar: *The Maratha Supremacy*, p. 407.
99. J.N. Sarkar: *op. cit.*, Vol. IV, p. 230.
100. *Ibid.*, p. 230.
101. *Ibid.*, p. 231.
102. *Ibid.*, p. 232.
103. *Ibid.*, p. 232; Francklin; *op. cit.*, p. 2; *Hissar District Gazetteer*, pp. 27-29.
104. J.N. Sarkar: *op. cit.*, p. 232.
105. Letter dated 31st August 1976, *Fort-William—Indian House Correspondence,* Vol. XVIII, p. 115.
106. J.N. Sarkar; *op. cit.*, p. 233.
107. *Ibid.*, p. 233.
108. Francklin: *op. cit.*, p. 22; J.N. Sarkar mentions his name as Ganga Vishnu, *see* p. 233.
109. Francklin; *op. cit.*, pp. 27-28.
110. *Ibid.*, pp. 27-28.
111. *Ibid.*, pp. 31.
112. For detail *see* Francklin: *op. cit.*, p. 31; In *Fort-William—Indian House Correspondence*, Vol. XVIII, the event has been given as below: A desertion of two battalions of Sepoys in the service of the Begum widow of Samroo having taken place, in consequence of hsr husband, Mr. Le Vassoull attempting to supersede the officer-in-command of them in favour of his nephew, this corps marched front their station near Delhi to that city; and put themselves under the orders of Zuffer Yaar Khan, the son of Samru by a former wife, whom the Begum has excluded from the succession to his father's *jagir*, in consequence of this revolt, the Begum and her husband quitted Surdunna and fled towards the Mahratta districts,, but were pursued and soon over-taken, and Mr. Le Vassoull finding he could not escape, shot himself. The Begum was carried

back a prisoner to Surdunna and Zuffer Yaar Khan who also proceeded thither on being informed of the above events is we conclude, now in possession of the *jagir*. *See* letter to the Courts of Directors, 9th January, 1796, p. 174.

113. Francklin: *op. cit.*, p. 35; Harbert Compton: *A Particular Account to European Military Adventurers of Hindustan* 1784-1803, (Karachi, 1976), p. 119.
114. J.N. Sarkar: *op. cit*, p. 234; R.C. Majumdar: *The Mahratha Supremacy*, p. 418; Francklin: *op. cit.*, p. 48.
115. L.H. Griffin has wrongly mentioned his name as Bawa Rao, see *The Rajas of the Punjab*, p. 81.
116. J.N. Sarkar: *op. cit.*, p. 234.
117. *Ibid.*, p. 236.
118. *Ibid.*, pp. 234-36.
119. Harbert Compton: *op. cit.*, p. 139.
120. J.N. Sarkar: *op. cit.*, p. 251.
121. H.G. Keen: *op. cit.*, p. 237.
122. L.H. Griffin: *The Rajas of the Punjab*, p. 81.
123. These fourteen paraganas were as follows: Hansi, Banwala, Tohana, Jamaudpur, Augrowa, Hissar, Behra, Seedreek, Svance, Tosham, Meham, Safidon, Jind and Kafahan.
124. L.H. Griffin: *The Rajas of the Punjab*, p. 82.
125. N K. Sinha: *Rise of the Sikh Power* (Calcutta, 1960), p. 95; J.N. Sarkar: *op. cit.*, p. 240; Francklin: *op. cit.*, p. 212.
126. J.N. Sarkar; *op. cit.*, p. 240.
127. *Ibid.*, p. 241.
128. *Ibid.*, p. 243.
129. L.H. Griffin: *The Rajas of the Punjab*, p. 88.
130. Miles Irving writes: "George Thomas, the Irish sailar who reigned at Hansi and aspired to conquer the Punjab, sleeps at Berhampur in Bengal." *See* Miles Irving: *List of Inscriptions on Tombs or Monuments in the Punjab, N.W.F. Provinces, Kashmir and Afghanistan*, Vol. VII, (Lahore, 1910), p. 2.
131. P.C. Roy Chaudhry : George Thomas : Haryana's Irish King, *Haryana Review*, Vol. XIII, No. 7 (July, 1979), p. 33.
132. J.D. Cunningham: *op. cit.*, p. 114.
133. Prabha Chopra: *op. cit.*, pp. 52-53.
134. Buddha Prakash: *Haryana Through the Ages*, p. 87.
135. *Ibid.*, p. 88.
136. J.N. Sarkar: *op. cit.*, Vol. IV, p. 337.

2

Haryana under the East India Company (1803-1857)

The Company's Attitude

Though the East India Company had already shown keen interest and appointed Major James Browne[1] as early as 1782 as their Agent at Delhi, but their motive was limited.[2] It was only to coilect secret information about the Delhi court. With the occupation of Delhi, the British Residency came into existence for the first time on September 24, 1803.[3]

Now the British had become the masters. David Ochterlony a 'tall and pleasing-looking man'[4] with 'military talents and experience'[5] was appointed as the first acting Resident and Chief Commandant with a garrison of one battalion and four companies of native infantry and a corps of Mewattis. In fact the Resident was the *de facto* authority of the East India Company. He was a magistrate, judge, collector, all united in one. He had two to four officials as his Assistants. The Marathas were deprived of all their rights in Haryana region with the treaty of Surji-Anjangaon,[6] and these privileges were bestowed upon the British. Due to its geographical proximity, this region was tagged with the Delhi Residency.

In the beginning the British were not so much keen in extending their influence in this region. However, they were conscious of its strategic situation, It could prove a barrier for any foreign attack from the side of the Indus. So they wanted to utilize it as a buffer state. But they could not remain neutral as some of the refractory *zamindars* and chiefs of the region threatened the security of the adjoining British territory.[8]

In the meanwhile Colonel William Scott was appointed to succeed Ochterlony as the Resident on February 25, 1804. He was very liberal in outlook. He submitted a proposal before joining at Delhi, to finalise the British relations with the Mughal Emperor. He advocated that a high degree of respect should be shown to the Emperor besides the payment of a sum not less than 36 lakhs of rupees annually for the expenses. He also advocated that the Emperor might be allowed to retain the control of his former possessions under the superintendence and control of the British Resident at his court. But Scott could not join his duty as he died on September 27, 1804, while on his way to Delhi from Lucknow.

Now David Ochterlony was confirmed as the Permanent Resident on November 7, 1804. Contrary to Mr. Scott, Ochterlony suggested only an annual payment of ₹ 1,55,500 to the Emperor and a sum of ₹ 10,000 on all important festivals. Similarly, he opposed the view of assigning any territory to the Emperor.[9] General Lake had the same opinion. But the Supreme Government at Calcutta was in favour of assigning the territory to the Emperor. Ochterlony further insisted that at least the control of the assigned territories should vest with the Resident.[10] Finally, his proposal was accepted.[11]

David Ochterlony on the day of his confirmation as Permanent Resident at Delhi suggested two means to create peace and order and harmony, and to suppress the refractory chiefs in Haryana. He recommended the assignment of the whole territory to the four prominent chiefs—Sahib Singh of Patiala, Bhag Singh of Jind, Jaswant Singh of Nabha and Bhai Lal Singh of Kaithal. Secondly, he proposed the complete establishment of British control over those territories from which the revenue was collected by the Marathas.[12]

But the East India Company did not want to entangle itself in the internal affairs and decided to take only military precautions for the defence of the British territory without establishing any direct control over those territories.[13] Consequently, as it was explained earlier, a part of territory on the right bank of the Jamuna was placed under the administration of the Resident as 'assigned territory' and the rest were given to the different chiefs and sardars.[14]

In January 1806 Archibald Seton was appointed as the Resident of Delhi, with Charles Metcalfe as his Assistant. The former was courteous, polite, lenient and kind hearted man. Like Lord Minto, the Governor-General of India, he was a staunch adherent of the policy of non-intervention. Ochterlony resented his own removal[15] and even Lord Lake, his mentor, requested Lord Minto to reconsider Ochterlony's case,[16] but in vain. Perhaps Ochterlony had become the victim of the prevailing official opinion that the high civil post should not be filled by the Military officers.[17] Seton assumed his duty on June 25, 1806.[18]

The withdrawal of the Marathas and the policy of non-intervention adopted by the British in the beginning created a political vacuum and it further created anarchy and confusion in the Haryana region. It encouraged ambitious Maharaja Ranjit Singh to fill the gap. He made three attacks during 1806-1808 on this region on one pretext or the other.

Internally, the mutual aggrandizement, rivalries, internal dissensions and discord'[19] and the 'political development in Europe in the early nineteenth century'[20] externally, provided an opportunity the British administration to change its attitude. In fact, the internal factors were not new. The Treaty of Tilsit in 1807 and the expectation of a joint attack by Napoleon and Tsar against the India alarmed the British administrators. There was also a possibility of a triple alliance among France, Turkey and Persia for the invasion of India.

The above external factors compelled Lord Minto, the Governor-General of India, and Seton to review their policy towards the chiefs. Consequently, Lord Minto sent missions to Persia, Afghanistan and Punjab to make friendly treaties. He also gave thought to the appeals of the *cis*-Sutlej chief for protection against the designs of Ranjit Singh which were previously refused on the principles of non-intervention. Charles Metcalfe was deputed to Punjab. Soon, with the efforts of Charles Metcalfe, the Treaty of Amritsar[21] was concluded on April 25, 1809, between the British and Ranjit Singh, by which the latter accepted the river Sutlej as the boundary of his territory and assured not to commit encroachment on the right of *cis*-Sutlej states. Consequently, a proclamation was issued to all the *cis*-Sutlej states on May 2, 1809 by which the latter came under the British protection.

In May 1811, Charles Theophilus Metcalfe[22] became the third Resident of Delhi. fie was a wise,[23] full of patience, liberal and a man of independent character and conduct.[24] He was a staunch supporter of Welleseleyian School and was a severe critic of the policy of non-intervention. To him it was impolitic, inexpedient and unjust.[25] Though Lord Minto had already deviated from his own policy of non-intervention in *cis*-Sutlej states by the proclamation of May 2, 1809, again on August 22, 1811 another proclamation was made in which the chief were forbidden from forcibly taking possession of the territories of others.

But with the appointment of Lord Moira (later Marques of Hastings) as Governor-General of India on October 14, 1813, the policy of non-intervention were completely changed. Metcalfe, the Delhi Resident now felt more comfortable as his views were equally shared by the Governor-General.

Metcalfe now paid attention not only the refractory chiefs but towards the whole region to maintain peace and tranquility. He introduced a novel system of administration—the Delhi system—a combination of native practice and the regulation spirit.[26] It was the confirmations of custom and the changes.[27] In the broader sense he was the first British administrator who studied the complicated problems of the region seriously and minutely. He studied the composition, the functions and the importance of the village communities and village Panchayats in the rural set up of the region. He admired very much their self-sufficient character and called the village Communities as 'little republics'.[28] He paid atttention towards the agrarian problems of the peasants like the system of land assessment, mode of revenue collection etc. He admired the judicious functions of the village Panchayats.

But in practice Metcalfe could not make any remarkable change. During his period the income from the land revenue was nearly doubled. While in 1811-12 it was only ₹ 9,87,030, 11.6, it increased in 1817-18 to ₹ 17,23,691.00.[29] Mode of collection also remained vigorous and ruthless.

In the sphere of criminal and civil justice he made certain fruitful achievements. He tried to suppress dacoity or gang-robbery. But he faced the difficulty from refractory territories adjoining the Delhi and the long-established habits of the Villagers of sheltering the gangs. Similarly, in the civil justice he paid attention towards the dispute about land and debts, and relied upon the existing Panchayats. But here also, he could not make any mark in the judicial system. On the contrary, he, at times, passed arbitrary judgements.[31] His system was attacked for the heavy sentences imposed by Metcalfe especially in crimes such as night robbery.[32]

In short while Metcalfe's Delhi system was admired by his successor Thomas Fortescue, in his Report of 1820 and it was considered to be Metcalfe's chief administrative achievement, it was vehemently criticised, on the basis of heavy sentences, by Mr. Even, a Member of the Commission of the Western Provinces, which was set up in 1823 to examine the Delhi Judicial System.[34] In 1829 Colebrooke accused Metcalfe of having started a system of jobbery and corruption at the Residency and in 1839 John Lawrence criticised him for the gross over-assessment.

However in 1819 after the departure of Metcalfe from Delhi, some frequent changes were made in set-up during 1819-1833. In 1819 the political and civil affairs of the Resident were divided between the Resident and the Commissioner respectively. The assigned territory was divided into three divisions (*i*) Northern Division, including Panipat, Sonepat, Rohtak, Hansi and Hissar; (*ii*) Central Division including the city of Delhi and its environs; and (*iii*) Southern Division including Palwal, Hodel, Mewat, Gurgaon and Rewari. Ail the three divisions were kept under Assistant Commissioners. Ochterlony was appointed as Resident and Forstescue as Commissioner. In the succeeding year, the latter's post redesignated as 'Deputy Superintendent' in place of the Commissioner and he was kept under the control of the Resident.

In May 1822, the Board of Revenue for the Western Provinces took over the administration of the territory. It was to give more efficiency and promptness in the administration. It was composed of three members namely Ross, Elliot and Fraser. In 1825 the civil administration was again bestowed on the Resident. But in 1829 it was again divided as it was. During this period except Sir Charles Metcalfe, who served as Resident during 1825-1827 for the second time, no man seriously served this territory. Other Residents during this period were H.S. Middleton, A. Ross, William Fraser,[37] C. Elliot Edward Colebrooke[38] etc., each of whom served for acouple of months. On Nov. 25, 1830, W.B. Martin, another significant Resident of Delhi was appointed.

In November 1834 the Agra Residency (the North-western Provinces since Feb. 29, 1836) was formed with Agra as its headquarters. Haryana had become one of its six divisions namely the Delhi Division.[39] The latter division included the districts of Panipat, Hissar, Delhi, Rohtak and Gurgaon consisting of 3,333 villages.[40] It remained a part of the North-western Provinces till the end of the East India Company, and the proclamation of Queen Victoria of November 2, 1858 at Allahabad by Lord Canning, the first Viceroy of British Crown. The administration of the present districts of Karnal, Kurukshetra and Ambala was under the control of the Superintendent of the Political Affairs and Agents to the Government in the territory of the protected Sikhs and Hill chiefs at Ambala.[41] Later the whole Haryana region was tagged with the Punjab administration in 1858.

Keeping in view the above historical survey of the administration during 1803-1858, one question may be asked that why the Haryana region including Delhi could not become the seat of authority. Why the Haryana region was again tagged with the North-western provinces? In fact, it was not only due to geographical proximity as it was attached in 1803 with Delhi. Perhaps the explanation requires a critical study of the period.

Firstly, the British authorities since their control of Delhi, including Haryana region, were conscious of the unique position of Delhi which was regarded as the symbolic seat of the sovereignty of India. As early as in 1803 Lord Welleseley had suggested the removal of the Emperor to Monghyr.[42] During 1803 to 1833 there were planned efforts on the part of the British authorities at Fort William at Calcutta and at Delhi to diminish the position and status of the Mughal emperor on various levels. Even Charles Metcalfe vehementally opposed the conciliatory attitude of the successors of Lord Welleseley.[43]

Lord Hastings was equally eager to end the pretentions of the emperor. During his period he took a number of steps, to lower the position of the emperor. For example, he refused the meeting with the latter except on a footing of equality'. He abolished Delhi Mint in 1818, though, the coin of the Company continued to bear its name till 1835. He also discouraged any communication between the emperor and the rulers of Indian States.

Lord Amherst and Lord William Bentinck also adopted the same attitude. Even the Mission of Raja Ram Mohan Roy to the

King of England regarding the royal stipend, could not bear any fruit. Undermining the position of the emperor, in a sense was an effort to diminish the unique position of Delhi and its adjoining areas. So it can be said that the Haryana region also became the victim of the revengeful attitude of the British.

Secondly, it was the mismanagement of the area by the British authorities which compelled Lord William Bentinck, the Governor-General of India, to transfer it to the Agra Presidency. His Minute of March 30, 1832 on the affairs of Rajputana and Delhi clearly gives his views on the issue. He wrote :

> "The administration of the Delhi has long been with me the subject of serious, and I must add, unsatisfactory reflection. It is difficult to conceive a system apparently more indefensive than by which the powers of judge, magistrate and collector are United under one individual, the officers possessing these extensive powers not only specially accepted from the control of the general regulations of our government, but not made subject to any other rule whatever and simply directed to proceed in the spirit of the regulations."[45]

The gravity of the situation can be fully gleaned from the following observation of the Governor-General:

> "In fact there is no law. The people are at the mercy and caprice of their immediate superior, who is often times a very young assistant, with little knowledge and discretion, and perfectly disqualified for so great a trust."[46]

Even the Court of Directors in their Despatch of the Nov. 17, 1830,[47] did not consider the administration of justice in the Delhi territories to have been placed on a satisfactory footing.

So, Lord William Bentinck suggested[48] a number of modifications before the creation of the Agra Presidency. The tribunal of appeal in revenue and judicial affairs was placed under the Allahabad Sadar Court and Board.

Thirdly, one more argument may be considered for the abolition of Delhi Presidency. With the planning to form a separate residency or agency at Rajputana, its abolition was pleaded on the ground of economy.[49]

Keeping in view the above circumstances and the subsequent events, it is clear enough that the British authority was not in favour of having the seat of authority at Delhi partly due to the possibility of the increasing of influence of the Mughal emperor and partly the unsatisfactory administrative set up of Delhi territory. Furthermore, it was accepted as a economic device.

The People's Response

Now let us have a glance at the reaction of the people of Haryana to the change of masters. There is no doubt that with the establishment of the rule of the East India Company in Haryana by the treaty of Surji Anjangaon, the period of "Great Anarchy" began to recede. The people treated them like other invaders—internal or external and continued their resistance wherever possible.

The Sikh chiefs of Ambala, Karnal and Thanesar were the first to oppose the Company rule. They formed a loose confederacy under Gurdit Singh ofLadwa and Bhanga Singh of Thanesar. But Bhag Singh of Jind and Lal Singh of Kaithal soon surrendered to General Lake. The Sikhs plundered and looted the Doab. Ochterlony, the Resident of Delhi, sent a big force under Colonel Burn in 1805 to subdue these Sikhs. The Sikhs first fought but soon left the field with the lone exception of Gurdit Singh of Ladwa. But he was also defeated in April 1805 at Karnal.[50] A part of his Jagir *i.e.* the *paraganas* of Karnal, was confiscated.[51] However the Company did not occupy the conquered territory. It remained under the control of the original chiefs under the treaty of Surji Anjangaon.

The second opposition came from the inhabitants of the Southern Haryana which included the districts of Gurgaon and Mahendergarh. These territories were ruled by the Company either directly or through some native chiefs. The local population mainly constituted of Meos, Ahirs, Jats and Ranghars who opposed the changed set up. According to C.T. Metcalfe.

> "They did not pay land revenue; nor they pay any other tax. No official, high or low, could afford to visit their villages without a company of infantry moving with him for his protection, and even then he was threatened with destruction."[52]

Anyhow, the people fought beyond their expectations. The Company had to make serious efforts to subdue them and by 1809 the British forces could crush their rebellion.

Similarly, the Muslim Bhatti Rajput of the western Haryana took a tough attitude. They organised under the leadership of Zabita Khan of Sirsa and Rania and Khan Bahadur Khan of Fatehabad. The British Government sent several expeditions to subdue the people. In order to rout the Bhattis and their leaders, a number of attacks were made. The British put a strong garrison at Hansi fort under the command of Mirza Illahi Beg, who was appointed as *Nazim* of Hissar. But he was killed by the people. The British distributed the above mentioned territory among the nawabs of Jhajjar, Loharu and Dujana. Now the British sent Colonel Browning, but the Bhattis again defeated the British forces. In the battle Colonel Browning was also killed. Another expedition was sent in 1809 under Colonel Ball,[55] but in vain. At last in November 1809 Colonel Adams was sent with a big contingent. He attacked Fatehabad, Sirsa and Rania on 3rd, 19th and 21st December, 1809 respectively. Colonel Adams won all the battles during this expedition. Khan Bahadur Khan and Zabita Khan both fled away from the battlefield. Anyhow, both the leaders were treated sympathetically. The Jagir of the latter was restored to him and the former was given a pension of ₹ 1,000 annually in lieu of his *jagir* of Fatehabad.

The Jats and Ranghars of Bhiwani territory challenged the authority. All the prominent rulers, Nawab Bahadur Khan, Ahmad Baksh Khan and Abdus Samad Khan had proved incompetent. There occurred a time when no body was willing to be the ruler of the area. The people were unwilling to brook anybody's overlordship. At last Archibold Seton, Resident at Delhi sent Garder, Assistant to the Resident, with a force of four battallions of infantry and a regiment of cavalry. He was accompanied by James Skinner with a cavalry force. They marched through Rohtak, Hissar and captured Bhiwani. To maintain peace and order the Hansi fort was converted into a military cantonment. Later in 1818 the military force was transferred to Bhadwas near Rewari.

From 27th to 29th August 1818 fierce battles took place. But on the last day the people of Bhiwani could not maintain their position and were compelled to retreat. The loss on both sides was considerable. On the British side one officer, 18 persons were killed and 120 wounded, on the other side about one thousand died.[53]

The British also paid their attention towards the native chiefs and sardars in the *cis*-Sutlej tract. The Government changed the policy of keeping the Yamuna as the boundary of their kingdom on the north-west. It was perhaps due to the serious danger of the intrusions of external powers like the French, the Turks and the Persians and the Russians into India which were mediating with Maharaja Ranjit Singh.[54] The frequent attacks of Maharaja Ranjit Singh, as has been mentioned earlier, during 1806-1808 made the British cautious, Frightened with the Ranjit Singh's September aggression,[55] the chiefs of Ladwa, Kaithal, Jind and Diwan of Patiala proceeded to Delhi in March 1808 to seek the British protection. They met Seton and secured protection through the proclamation of May 2, 1809.

So it can be said that by the end of the first decade of the 19th century the British had Consolidated their position in Haryana and had become the real masters of the territory.[56]

Revolt of Jodh Singh of Kalsia for Chhachrauli 1810-18

Though the British controlled the Delhi territory in 1809-10, the opposition did not completely subside. The mismanagement and the absence of judicial administration, coercive methods adopted for the land settlement and maltreatment of the chiefs by the British encouraged antagonism between the rulers and the ruled. A series of disturbances and revolts took place during the East India Company's tenure.

First of all, it was the Chhachrauli disturbances. Bungaila Singh, the chief of the petty State of Chachhrauli (now a part of Jagadhari Tehsil in Ambala District), died in 1809. He did not have any male issue. Jodh Singh, the chief of Kalsia, one of the Krorasinghia-misls, occupied Chhachrauli.[57] David Ochterlony, opposed his action and demanded his immediate withdrawal so that the state might be given to Rani Ram Kaur, the widow of Bungaila Singh. Ochterlony also threatened to launch an attack. Consequently, Jodh Singh withdrew his forces in 1810.

But Jodh Singh did not permanently give up his ambitious designs. In 1818 he reoccupied the territory. The British authorities sent Brigadier-General Arnold with heavy troops in October 1818. Meanwhile, Rani Ram Kaur became unpopular among her subjects due to her mismanagement. People, instead of helping her cooperated with Jodh Singh. But Jodh Singh could not retain his position and was compelled to retreat again. The Chhachrauli State was now annexed to the British territory.[58]

Prince Pratap Singh of Jind, Bewari 1814-16

Raja Bhag Singh the ruler of Jind suffered a paralytic stroke in March 1813.[59] Now it became necessary to think of his successors.[60] The Raja wished to appoint his younger son Pratap Singh as his successor. But the British Agent favoured the rule of promogenature and showed his support to the elder son Fateh Singh. Anyhow, the Draft Will of Raja Bhag Singh was forwarded by Colonel Ochterlony, to the Resident at, Delhi for transmission to the Government of India.[61] The British Government declared Pratap Singh as incompetent for succession.[62] Rani Sobrahi, the mother of the third son, Mehtab Singh was appointed as regent in 1814.

Consequently Pratap Singh revolted on 23rd June 1814. He occupied the Jind fort on 23rd August, 1814 and put to death the Rani Sobrahi, her main adviser Munshi Jaishi Ram, the Commander of the fort and others.[63] Sir Charles Metcalfe, the Resident of Delhi, soon despatched troops under Colonel Arnold against him.

Pratap Singh left Jind and reached Balawali fort. However he was followed by a contingent of the British cavalry. After a circular march, Pratap Singh crossed Sutlej and reached Makhowal, where he was joined by Phula Singh Akali with his forty followers, about seven hundred horses and two guns.[64] He remained there for two months. After a short stay he came back in Balawali fort, where he was compelled to surrender on 28th January, 1815 and was taken prisoner. He was kept under nominal restraint. However, in the course of his march to Delhi, he managed to escape and fled to Lahore in the vain hope of getting an asylum from Ranjit Singh. He was kept in confinement and died in June 1816.[65]

Strained relations of Sangat Singh with the British 1826-34

Sangat Singh, 11 years old son of Fateh Singh became Raja on 30th July 1822 at Jind. He made friendly relations with Maharaja Ranjit Singh. He visited Lahore twice in 1826 and 1827 respectively.[66] He was given a number of Jagirs like *trans*-Sutlej, Rai Majara, Maheranpur, Masupur etc.[67] These concessions roused the suspicion of British authorities. To escape from the eyes of the British authorities, Sangat Singh went to live in a town eighty miles away[68] from Jind. In fact it encouraged confusion and disorder. Robbery, dacoities, outrages were committed frequently.[69]

In 1834 Sangat Singh again visited Lahore, 'which infuriated the British and they censored him for his unauthorised negotiations with the Lahore Court[70]. But he died suddenly on 2nd Nov. 1834. As the deceased Raja had no issue, the British Government at first thought of annexing the whole state of Jind but later postponed the idea.[71] However, the British Government forfeited a part of Sangat's estate.[72] Later, Sarup Singh, cousin of Sangat Singh, was formally installed in April 1837.

Revolt of Gulab Singh and Dal Singh at Balawali 1835-46

With the death of Sangat Singh of Jind the territory of Balawali was also annexed by the British Government. But the people of the area resented it vigorously, under the leadership of Gulab Singh Gill, an ex-*Resaldar* of Jind Army and Dal Singh, brother-in-law of Prince Pratap Singh. Perhaps Mai Sul Rani, the widow of Pratap Singh instigated them. A British army was sent to suppress the rebels. Due to the absence of better arms and ammunitions the people had to suffer heavy casualties. Gulab Singh was killed and Dal Singh and Mai Sul Rani were arrested and imprisoned.

Murder of William Fraser and its effects

William Fraser, earlier Member of the Board of Revenue, was the Resident of Delhi since 1830. He was very much unpopular among the masses. It is said that he was oppressive, cruel and licentious. Even Sir Charles Metcalfe considered him to be "self-willed to such a great extent that no power could be entrusted to him without some risk of its being abused."[73] He was murdered on March 22, 1835.

Two versions were prevailing regarding his murder. Firstly, Shamasuuddin Khan, tbe Nawab of Ferozepur-Jhirka and Loharu, did not want to pact of his territory for the maintenance of his two brothers, Amin-ud-din and Jiaud-ud-din, as desired by their father, Ahmad Bakhsh. Fraser instigated his brothers to get their due.[74] Consequently it created enemity between the Nawab and Fraser.

Second version attributes the murder to the licentious character of Fraser, who went to the extent of seducing[75] the beautiful cousin of Nawab Shamsu-ud-din who respected Fraser like an elder brother.

Anyhow, it is clear that Nawab Shamasu-ud-din conspired against Fraser who was shot dead by Karim Khan, *Daroga-i-Shikar* of the former. Later Shamasu-ud-din and Karim Khan were tried and sentenced to death.[76] In fact, what was alarming for the British Government was not the murder itself, but the proceedings of the Court which roused immense popular interest. In fact, both of them became heroes in the eyes of the public.

Karim Khan was hanged on 28th August 1835. The day was observed as a sacred day. He was called *Gul-i-Shahid*. Special prayers were observed in mosques in Delhi. Similarly Nawab was hanged on 8th October, 1835. Nearly 8,000 people witnessed his gallows at Delhi between Kashmiri Gate and Mori-Gate.

Their trials also gave impetus to the mobilization of the public opinion, which gave birth to the Urdu Press.[77] *The Delhi Akhbar* was published in 1836, followed by *Sayyad-ul-Akhbar* (1837), *Siraj-ul-Akhbar* (1841), *Karim-ul-Akhbar* (1845), *Quran-us-Sadan* (1845) and *Sadiq-ul-Akhbar* (1853) etc.[78]

Reyolt of Mehtab Kanr of Kaithal 1842-43

Bhai Udai Singh, the Chief of Kaithal died on the 15th March 1843 without any heir. He had two wives, Suraj Kaur, daughter of the Raja of Ballabhgarh and Mehtab Kaur, daughter of a *Zamindar*. Suraj Kaur died shortly after the state lapsed. Mehtab Kaur lived for some years. She was a brave lady.

Now a small portion of the territory yielding an amount of one lakh of rupees per annum was given to Bhai Gulab Singh of Arnowali, who was the second cousin of Bhai Gurbaksh Singh, the great grandfather of the chief. While the main territory including Kaithal, worth about 4 lakhs of rupees per annum, was confiscated by the British Government.

The Phulkian chiefs—the Raja of Patiala, Nabha and Jind protested against this act and requested Mr. Greathed, the special British Agent at Kaithal, to transfer the possession of the state to them, as it belonged to their family. But the Government refused to oblige them. The British invaded Kaithal on April 10, 1843, but in vain. They tried again to capture Kaithal on April 15. Mehtab

Kaur, meanwhile left Kaithal. The decisive battle was fought near the present Jat School.[79] The news letter on the Kaithal conquest was sent to Queen Victoria. This is preserved at the British Museum, London. Henry Lawrence vividly described this area in his settlement Report in 1843. In fact, the annexation of Kaithal was against all canons of justice.[80]

Revolt of Ajit Singh of Ladwa 1845-46

Now Raja Ajit Singh of Ladwa became the victim of the British campaign of confiscation of territories. He was charged with corruption and mismanagement and his removal was suggested. In fact, his enemity towards the British was well-known. By 1845, he became intolerable to the British Government. Accordingly he was pronounced a 'rebel' and put under surveillance at Saharanpur.

During the First Anglo-Sikh war, Ajit Singh fled away from the Jail, joined the Sikh army and helped Ranjodh Singh Majithia. At Ludhiana, Ajit Singh and Ranjodh Singh burnt a portion of the cantonment.[81] Sir Harry Smith, who had taken part in the battle of Waterloo and was sent to help the British army against the Sikhs suffered a heavy loss of baggage—hospital stores at the hands of the Sikhs.[82] After the battle the estate of Ajit Singh was confiscated.

Hostile attitude of the Sikh Chiefs of the *Cis*-Sutlcj States 1845-50

During the first Sikh war the Sikh chiefs were asked to supply men, money and ammunition and helped the British against the *trans*-Sutlej Sikhs. Perhaps this was the first occasion for these states to fulfil their obligations contracted under the treaties made in 1809, but the Sikh-chiefs showed no eagerness. According to Griffin, "The Majority (of the smaller chiefs) had not shown their loyalty in 1845 in any more conspicuous way than in not joining the enemy." In fact they were 'passionately obstructed.'[83]

Consequently the Government deprived some of the chiefs of the authority vested in them. Some of the chiefs were removed and their lands confiscated.[84] The Raja of Rupar was deprived of his 106 villages. Similarly Sodhis of Anandpur lost 72 villages. Later in 1850 State of Thanesar was confiscated. In fact most of the chiefs were reduced to the position of ordinary *jagirdars*. Process of annexation and consolidation of the British empire extended frequently. Certain measures were adopted in the name of reforms, for example, the police jurisdiction in most of the States was abolished. The transit and custom duties were abolished. From March 1847 certain changes in legal procedure were made. It was made clear that the chiefs and their people were forced to be amenable to the British judicial courts. In June 1849, with a few exceptions, all the chiefs were deprived of all civil, criminal and fiscal jurisdiction. In this way the British extended their direct management to the *cis*-Sutlej territories which included a part of Haryana.

NOTES

1. Major James Browne acted as British Agent at Delhi during December 11, 1783 to April 22, 1785. For detail *see* Krishnan Dayal Bhargava (Ed): *Browne Correspondence* (New Delhi, 1960), pp. 1-5.
2. Percival Spear: *Twilight ofthe Mughals,* (Cambridge, 1951). p. 23.
3. Lake to Wellesley, Sept. 23, 1803 see *Secret Consultations,* March 2, 1804, No. 119.
4. Reginald Heber: *Narrative of Journey through the Upper Provinces of India,* Vol. II, (London, 1829), pp. 392-93.
5. K.N. Panikkar: *British Diplomacy in North India, A Study of Delhi Residency (1803-1857),* (New Delhi, 1968), p. 9.
6. C.U. Aitchison (Compl.): *Treaties, Engagements and Sanads,* Vol. IV, pp. 42-46.
7. K.N. Panikkar: *op. cit.,* p. 99.
8. Percival Spear: *op. cit.,* p. 85.
9. Ochterlony to Edmonston, Nov. 30, 1804; Ochterlony to Edmonston, December 1, 1804. see *Secret Consultations,* Jan. 31, 1805, No. 227; K.N. Panikkar, *op. cit.,* p. 13.
10. Ochterlony to Governor-General, Feb. 9, 1805, see *Secret Consultations,* March 28, 1805, No. 168.
11. Lumsden Chief Secretary to Ochterlony, May 22, 1805, *Secret Consultations,* June 20, 1805, No. 422; K.N. Panikkar: *op. cit.,* pp. 1-13.
12. Ochterlony to Edmonston, Nov. 7, 1804, *Secret Consultations,* Nov. 21, 1804, No. 306; Panikkar: *op. cit.,* p. 100.
13. Edmonston to Ochterlony, Jan. 13, 1805, *Secret Consultations,* Jan. 31, 1805, No. 243.
14. Buddha Prakash: *Haryana through the Ages,* p. 87.
15. Ochterlony to Lord Lake, Feb. 12, 1806 *Secret Consultations,* March 6, 1806, No. 2.
16. Lord Lake to G.G., Feb. 14, 1806, *Secret Consultations,* March 6, 1806, No. 1.
17. K.N. Panikkar: *op. cit.,* p. 19.
18. Seton to Edmonston, June 25, 1806; *Political Consultations,* July 17, 1806, No. 21.
19. K.N. Pannikar: *op. cit.,* p. 100.
20. *Ibid.,* p. 102.
21. For detail *see* Appendix I.

22. Sir Charles Metcalfe (1785-1846), born on 30th Jan., 1785 at Calcutta, son of Major Metcalfe, studied at Eton, reached Delhi in 1801, appointed assistant to the Resident at the Court of Sindhia, Political Assistant to Lord Lake in 1804, Assistant to the Resident at Delhi, went to the court of Maharaja Ranjit Singh and concluded a treaty on April 25, 1809, Resident at the Court of Sindhia in 1810, appointed Resident in Delhi in 1811, Political Secretary to the Governor-General, Resident at the Court of Nizam Hyderabad, Resident at Delhi in October 1825-27; Member of the Supreme Council 1827-34, awarded the title of 'Sir', appointed first Govemor of Agra Province and nominated Provisionally Governor-General of India, resigned in 1836, left India in 1838, Governor of Jamica 1842, Governor-General of Canada, died Sept. 5, 1846, known as the 'Liberator of the Indian Press': For detail see Panigrahi: *Charles Metcalfe in India* (Delhi, 1970); G.D. Oswell: *Sketches Rulers of India, The Company's Governors*, Vol., II, (First Ed., 1908) (Reprint, Delhi, 1972); J.W. Kaye : *Life of Lord Metcalfe*, 1854.
23. At the time of Treaty of Amritsar 1809 Maharaja Ranjit Singh once commented: 'If their beardless young men are so wise what must their old men lie': *See* G.D. Oswell: *op. cit.*, Vol. II, pp. 119-159.
24. *Ibid.*, p. 165.
25. Metcalfe to Edmonstone, June 20, 1811, *Political Consultations*, July 12, 1811, No. 1.
26. For detail *see* Panigrahi: *op. cit.*
27. Percival Spear: *op. cit.*, pp. 87-88.
28. C.F. Metcalfe: *Minute of the Board of Revenue*, 17 Nov. 1830. For the nature of the village community *see also* D.R. Gadgil: *The Industrial Evolution of India in Recent Times*, Calcutta, 1950; T.B. Desai: *Economie History of India under the British; Census Report*, 1901.
29. Panigrahi: *op. cit.*, p. 47; Percival Spear: *op. cit.*, p. 101.
30. Percival Spear: *op. cit.*, p. 92.
31. Panigrahi: *op. cit*, pp. 149-51.
32. Percival Spear: *op. cit.*, p. 99.
33. *Ibid.*, p. 98.
34. *Ibid.*, p. 99.
35. *Ibid.*, p. 100.
36. *Ibid.*, p. 101.
37. William Fraser (1784-1835), son of Edward Fraser, came in India in 1799; Secretary to Ochterlony in 1805, became Member of the Board of Revenue N. W.P., became Resident at Delhi in 1830. For detail *see* Percival Spear : *op. cit.*, pp. 182-93.
38. For detail of the Colebrooke case, *See* Percival Spear: *op. cit.*, pp. 168-81.
39. Dharm Bhanu: *History and Administration of the North Western Provinces (1803-1858)*, (Agra, 1957), p. 145.
40. Martin Montgomery: *The History of Indian Empire*, Vol. I, p. 514.
41. Farooqi: British Relations *with the cis-Sutlej States* (1809-1823), Punjab Govt. Monograph No. 19.
42. Wellesley to Lake, July 27, 1803, *Secret Consultations*, March 2, 1804, No. 6.

43. K.N. Pannikkar: *op. cit.*, p. 137.
44. *Ibid.*, pp. 138-42.
45. Bentinck's Minutes on the affairs of Rajputana and Delhi, 30 March 1832 vide C.H. Phillips (Ed.): *The Correspondence of Lord William Cavendish Bentinck (1832-35)*, Vol. II, (Oxford, 1977), p. 788.
46. *Ibid.*
47. *Ibid.*
48. *Ibid.*, p. 790.
49. *Ibid.*, Sir Charles Metcalfe to Bentinck, Calcutta 19th Jan. 1832, p. 759.
50. *Karnal District Gazetteer*, pp. 24-25.
51. J.D. Cunningham: *op. cit.*, p. 115.
52. Kaye: *Selections from the Papers of Charles Metcalfe*, Vol. I, p. 55.
53. Mill: *History of Political India*, Vol. VII, pp. 138-39.
54. J.D. Cunningham: *op. cit*, p. 123; Griffin and Massey: *The Punjab Chiefs and the Families of Note*, Vol. I, p. 54.
55. J.D. Cunningham: *op. cit.*, p. 122.
56. K.C. Yadav: Early Resistance to British Rule in Haryana (1803-1810), *Punjab History Conference, Proceedings*, (Ninth Session, 1975), p. 91.
57. Martin Montgomery: *op. cit.*, Vol. I, p. 522; J.D. Cunningham: *op. cit.*, p. 127.
58. J.D. Cunningham: *op. cit.*, p. 127.
59. L.H. Griffin: *The Rajas of the Punjab*, p. 338.
60. *Ibid.*
61. *Ibid.*, p. 339.
62. *Ibid.*, p. 343.
63. *Ibid.*, p. 344.
64. *Ibid.*, pp. 349-50.
65. *Ibid.*, p. 352.
66. *Ibid.*, p. 355.
67. *Ibid.*, pp. 356-57.
68. *Ibid.*, p. 359.
69. *Ibid.*
70. *Ibid.*, p. 360.
71. *Ibid.*, p. 363.
72. *Ibid.*, For detail *see* Table of Settlement of the Jind Possession, pp. 377-78.
73. Dr. Prabha Chopra: *op. cit.*, p. 56.
74. *Ibid.*
75. *Ibid.*
76. For detail of the tracing of this murder see R. Bosworth Smith: *The Life of Lord Lawrence*, (London, 1883); *see also* John Lawrence in Haryana (1831-35), *Journal of Haryana Studies*, Vol. III, No. 1, (Jan. 1971), pp. 17-20.
77. Dr. Prabha Chopra: *op, cit.*, p. 57.
78. *Ibid.*
79. S.C. Mittal ; Kaithal: Past and Present, *The Tribune*, 9-1-1977; Pandit Sunderlal: *Bharat Mein Angrazi Raj Ke Do So Varsh*; Desraj: *Panjab Ka Itihas*.

80. *See* Ganda Singh: *Private Correspondence Relating to the Anglo Sikh Wars.*
81. *Ibid.*, p. 96.
82. *Ibid.*
83. *Ibid.*, p. 67.
84. L.H. Griffin: *The Rajas of the Punjab*, p. 207.

3

The Uprisings of 1857 and the Aftermath

The Tension

On May 10, 1857, a great event which may be equated with the fall of Bastile, took place in the history of India. It was the great uprising which was started by the sepoys at Ambala and Meerut. Three days later, it spread throughout the country.

To call it a sudden affair resulting from introduction of new cartridges with cow's fat or pig's lard or 'a rebel in self-defence' due to the careless uttering of a 'cook boy' that the artillery and the rifles were to be snatched from the natives seems to be too simple an explanation of the whole happenings. In fact, as the sequence of events revealed that it was a premediated anti-British, patriotic but ill-organised effort.

In Haryana a number of factors contributed to its intensity and extensiveness. In short, firstly, the time honoured institutions like the village communities and the *panchayats* were abolished by the British. In fact these institutions were the centres of all the social and economic life of the villages which were characterised by self sufficiency, stability, the internai cohesion and the highly organised system of self-government.[2] Perhaps it was this peculiarly self-sufficient structure of the village that preserved the civilization of India through the many invasions and the many changes of rulers and Governments.[3] C.T. Metcalfe, as we have seen in the earlier chapter, highly praised the village communities and likened them to 'little republics'. Their abolition shook the faith and confidence of the people.

Secondly, the land policy adopted by the Company further up-set the life of the peasants or petty proprietors who were already poor. It stimulated a wider gulf between the British ruler and the peasants who constituted 90% of the total population. It was generally admitted by the British authorities that the early summary assessment of land revenue was oppressive and the methods of assessment and collection were vexatious and extortionate.[4] Consequently, it created tension among the peasantry. Some illustrations would be better for its clarification. In the then Hissar District, the demands for the three summary settlements for ten, five and ten years respectively during 1815 and 1840 were so high that full collections were the exceptions.[5] For example, the demand of the first settelement (1815-1825) was so high that it exceeded by 20% the revenue fixed in 1890 for the same village.[6] It was further increased in the two settlements.7 The demand for a tract in 1839 was 4.9 lakhs which in 1890 was assessed at only about 2/3 of it.[8] So this policy of heavy revenue greatly demoralised[9] the people and shattered the peasants economy. Similarly, in other districts it was harsh and unsympathetic.[10] In fact this oppressive policy compelled many of the peasants to desert their lands and homes.[11]

Some efforts were made to improve the land revenue system by Lord William Bentinck. In January 1833 he convened a meeting of the officials of the Revenue Department at Allahabad. Its proceedings led to the passing of the famous Regulation IX of 1833. Its aim was to improve the machinery for the revision of the land revenue. This Regulation was also implemented to the Delhi Division.[12] It based the assessment of land revenue on the amount of rent paid by the land-holders on the eve of the settlement instead upon the amount of the produce of the land as it was prevailing from the days of the Mughals.

Robert Martins Bird, a senior Member of the Board of Revenue at Allahabad, appointed a good team of settlement officers for the purpose. In Haryana people like John Lawrence, who later became the Viceroy of India were selected.

The settlement started in 1833 and in 1842. R.M. Bird submitted an incomplete but detailed report. During his nine years of hard work (1833-1842) he minutely studied the problem of the land assessment, its defects and needs of reforms. He admitted that the prevailing land revenue System was most defective, corrupt, excessive and harassing to the peasantry. He noted the defects of high assessment and short-term settlements[13] and considered that over assessment was economically unsound, likely to lead to huge arrears of revenue and the ultimate impoverishment of the peasantry.[14]

The Lieutenant-Governor accepted Bird's suggestions and observed in his Minute of December 1842, regarding Delhi Division:

> "It will be wise to obtain for some years to come such a demand as the people can pay without pressure, so as to encourage them to adopt habits of industry. A light assessment now will prove immediately beneficial for the tract of the country and eventually profitable to the state."[15]

R.M. Bird also suggested the necessity of irrigation of lands for the improvement and advancement of agriculture.[16] He himself wrote regarding Haryana region:

> ". . . No increase of resources can be expected from the Delhi territory on a revison of settlement unless the Government should hereafter open a canal."[17]

Bird also recommended a number of reforms. He dis- missed inefficient *patwaris*.[18] Hindi was to be adopted as the language of official transactions in place of Persian. The land revenue fixed to be collected in four instalments in place of eight or nine. He also suggested the imposition of cess for the construction of the roads and the creation of the village police.

In fact all these suggestions were vehementally opposed by the peasants. During 1833-1842 besides Karnal District and some part of the Gurgaon District, Bird assessed the land of the Delhi Division. But no significant difference was made from the former demand. Later T.C. Robertson and James Thomason,[19] the successive Lieutenant-Governors of the North-Western Provinces made certain suggestions and revised Bird's assessment. It was completed in 1849.

As regards the state share, according to Regulation VII of 1822 it was 83% of the gross rental or assets of the estates. In 1833 Lord William Bentinck reduced it to 66% of the gross rental. R.M. Bird and Robertson enforçed this rate of land revenue. Thomason also accepted it. In Rule 52 of the Thomason's code, he had fixed 66%

of the rental as the maximum limit. In fact, even the two third rent was very heavy. It racked the village economy and compelled to the peasants to mortgaged their property.

Even the construction of the western Yumna canal could not improve the economic conditions of the peasants due to heavy rates. From 1820 to 1846-47 the total water-rent collected from the canal was ₹ 35,47,643. While in 1820 it was only ₹ 876-4-0 in 1846-47 it had risen to ₹ 2,62,539,

The construction of the Yumna canal rather created some problems.[21] It was eventually followed by the accumulation of *reh* and silt deposit. At some places due to the above level of the canal from the land, it created difficulty of seepage and waterlogging resulting into a series of lagoons and stagnant marshes. Malaria became a serious health-hazard of Karnal and Panipat areas. Karnal which was a cantonment in 1806 later came to be a 'mausoleum for civilians'.[22]

The third significant factor of discontent was the frequent famines and epedemic which had worsened the condition of the people. While the *Chalisa* famine of 1783 completley ruined the Hissar District,[23] the famines of 1803-4, 1813-14, 1816-17, 1825-26, 1832-34 and 1837-38 severely affected the whole region. The terrible famine of 1803-4 was due to the scarcity of fodder and grain in which thousands of people and the cattle perished. The wheat price rose to seven seers for a rupee. In 1832-34 and 1837-38 the famines led to bread riots.[24] Similarly, the epedemic of 1841 and 1843 caused heavy casualties, and added fuel to the fire. In 1851-52 famine again visited Haryana. In fact the East India Company could not help the poor victims due to the absence of any definite policy in this regard.

Fourthly it is in the sphere of justice that the British administration lacked most. Before the advent of the British set up the administration of justice in Haryana as well as in other parts of India was very simple, cheap, prompt and impartial. The village *Panchayats* played a significant role in this sphere. These were the foundations of the Indian judicial set up. The decision of the village *Panchayats* were admitted as the voice of the God. But later these became out of date.

The British judicial set up was repressive, arbitary and 'expensive. Delay tactics were generally applied. There was no proper check on the judges and no provision for appeal. It was neither liked by the people of the country nor appreciated by the efficient and reasonable British administrators. Martin Montgomery wrote, "The inefficient administration of justice is an admitted evil. The costliness, the procrastination, above all, the perjury and corruption made over civil and criminal courts notorious."[25] Even a utilitarian Governor-General of India like Lord William Bentinck had, vehementally criticised the prevailing System in his famous Minute of 30th March 1832 on the affairs of Rajputana and Delhi. He commented: "In fact there is no law. The people are at mercy and caprice of their immediate superior, who is often times a very young assistant, with little knowledge and discreation and perfectly disqualified for so great a trust..."[26] Even the Court concluded its remarks, "We cannot consider the administration of justice to have been hitherto placed on a satisfactory footing in the Delhi territories."[27]

The judicial system in Haryana which was a part of the north-western provinces suffered heavily throughout the Company's rule due to the absence of a complete set of Civil and Criminal laws, the wide spread prevailing bribery and corruption among the judges, more emphasis on technicalities than the spirit of the laws, absence of interest by the British authorities etc.[28] It can be said that the main principles upon which the administration was based were "despotism, high-handed corruption, inefficiency, judicial slackness and the terror of Police raj." As regards the judicial skelton set up after the control of the East India Company in 1810, it was divided into two categories. For the Delhi the highest authority was the Resident. There were three types of local courts under three Indian subordinate officers known as Qazi, Mufti and Pandit. For other parts of the Delhi territory, the District Officer was the authority in practically all the matters.[29]

Fifthly, it was the attack on their *Dharma* that made the people, the enemy of the British. The Christian missionaries started their campaign of conversion to Christianity. In these efforts they were actively supported by the British officials. They started the English schools, the dispensaries and the Gospel of the Christ. The first Bapatist Missionary in Delhi was John Chamberlain who visited Delhi in 1814 as tutor to the son of Begum Samru.[30] In 1818 a fulfledged Mission was set up. The Ludhiana American Presbytarian Mission had also started its branch at Ambala City and Ambala Cantonment. The Society for the propagation of the

Gospel was also started at Delhi. But these missions could not gain any considerable success in their conversion programme.

In towns and cities, these missionaries got some success. For example, Ram Chander (1821-1880), a Kayastha of Panipat, a teacher in Delhi College, Delhi, embraced christianity on 5th May 1852.[31] The news perturbed hundreds of Hindus and Muslims who condemned this action and criticised the Government attitude.[32]

Lastly, a large number of feudal chiefs and sardars could not forget their old good days. A number of estates had been confiscated by the British. For example, significant States like Rania and Chhachrauli, Ambala, Kaithal, Ladwa and Thanesar were permanently confiscated in the year 1818, and 1823, 1843, 1845, 1850 respectively. Doctrine of lapse created a sense of dissatisfaction and insecurity among the remaining chiefs. So it can be said at least in regard to Haryana, that the great uprising was partly due to the socio-economic discontent among the peasantry and partly to the dissatisfaction of the princes.

The influential leaders of the uprising in Haryana were mainly feudal chiefs like Rao Tula Ram of Rewari, Nahar Singh of Ballabhgarh, Ahmed Ali of Farrukhnagar, Abdur Rehman of Jhajjar, Bahadurjang Khan of Dadri, Hasan Ali of Dujana, and Nur Mohamad Khan of Rania and Ammuddin of Loharu and Akbar Ali of Pataudi.

The Tussle

Keeping in view the causes of the general discontentment, it would be necessary to have a brief survey of the great uprising district-wise in Haryana.[33] According to a private letter of a British Officer dated 14 May 1857, at about 9.00 a.m. on 10th May 1857 the 60th N.I. (Native Infantry) Stationed at Ambala initiated the revolt.[34] Later the 5th N.I. also joined them. But the prompt action on the part of the British saved their position. Similarly, on the 10th the sepoys at Meerut also revolted. The latter reached Delhi on the 11th at 7.00 a.m.

Delhi, the grand capital of the Mughal emperor, a city of nearly 152,000 population[35] took the uprising by surprise.[36] The rumour was that the Russians had come. Even the king[37] knew nothing earlier. Later the 38th Regiment, which was on duty joined the coming troops. Some of the British and Anglo-Indians were murdered. The British rule in Delhi was destroyed in a couple of davs.[38]

From Delhi the news of the uprising spread throughout the Haryana region. Nearly 300 sepoys from Delhi reached Gurgaon. They were joined by the people and a few feudal chiefs, like Nawab Ahmed Mirza Khan and Nawab Duala Jan. W. Ford, the Collector-Magistrate of Gurgaon tried to suppress the revolt but failed.[39] Consequently, he fled to Mathura *via* Palwal along with some European officials.

In Mewat the people under the leadership of Sadruddin, a Meo peasant of Pinnghwa, revolted against the British regime. The first target were the loyalists who were murdered. The rebels looted Tauru, Sohna, Ferozepur-Jhirka, Punhana and Pinnghwa. At Nuh the loyalists gave a stiff fight but failed. Similarly, near Hodal and Hathin, the loyal Rawat jats and the Rajputs of Hathin were beaten at the hands of Surot jats of Hodal and Pathans of Seoli.[40] All the efforts by the British to suppress the revolt and help the loyalists failed. Even Major W. F. Eden, the political agent at Jaipur, who reached Mewat with a big contingent consisting nearly seven thousand soldiers could not move towards Delhi.[41] Owing to the revolt, he had to return to Jaipur.

In Ahirwal, Rao Tula Ram and his cousin Gopal Dev struggled and captured Rewari. Tula Ram established not only his own administration[42] but also helped Bahadurshah, who confirmed him in his *Jagirs* of Rewari, Bhora-Kalan, and Shahjahanpur.[43] Similarly at Palwal, Faridabad, Bahadurgarh and Farukhanagar the people revolted against the British rule.

But, since the month of October, the British Government succeeded in turning the tide. On October 2, 1857 Bregadier General Showers marched towards Gurgaon with a force of 1,500 men, a light field battery, 18 twopounder-guns and two small mortars.[44] His aim was to crush the Gujars, Mewatis, Ranghars, Ahirs and the rebel feudal chiefs. Reaching at Rewari, he captured the mud fort of Rampura and asked Tula Ram for submission which he bluntly refused. But in a short period he was subdued and the British captured the forts of Jhajjar (17 October) Dadri (19 October) Kanod (19 October) Farukhanagar (21 October) and Ballabhgarh (2l October), Nawabs of Jhajjar and Dadri and Farukhanagar were arrested and sent to Delhi.

Though Showers gained some success but during the period he faced a number of rebellions. For example, near Sohna the villagers attacked his troops and killed about 60 of them. In fact, he could not capture the prominent leaders of the revolt like Rao Tula Ram.

After a couple of days the British authorities were again alarmed by the concentration of the rebels at Rewari and Narnaul. On 10th November, 1857, a big force was sent under Colonel Gerrard. On 13th November he captured Rampura (Rewari) and reached Nasibpur near Narnaul on 15th November. Here the rebels attacked him. In fact, it was a blunder on the part of the rebels to have become impatient and take to offence in place of defence.[45] Perhaps, it was one of the most decisive battles of the uprising of 1857[46] so far as the Haryana region is concerned. In this battle 70 British soldiers were killed and 45 wounded. They lost their Commander Colonel Gerrard and Captain Wallace. Lieutenants Craige, Kennedy and Pearse were wounded. On the Indian side, Rao Kishan Singh, Ramlal and General Samad Khan's son were killed. Anyhow Rao Tula Ram and General Samad Khan escaped.

The Mewatis continued their struggle. They plundered the Government treasuries and attacked the loyalists. Captain Drummond, the incharge of Sohna and Tauru area, receiving the alarming news, proceeded to Rupraka. He burnt all the Meo villages on the Sohna-Rupraka road. At Rupraka nearly 400 Meos lost their lives.

To suppress the revolt in Mewat, Clifford, the Assistant Collector of Gurgaon made sternous effort. He burnt many villages and murdered the inhabitants. Perhaps he was in a revengeful mood,[47] as his sister had been insulted, humiliated and murdered at Delhi in the presence of the Emperor's son. Later he was murdered by the Meos.

On 27th November 1857 Captain Ramsay reached the village of Pinnghwa to check the activity of the rebel leader Sadruddin. A number of Meos including the son of Sadruddin Were killed, but Sadruddin escaped.

Like the Meos of Gurgaon, the Ranghars of Rohtak District played a significant role. The leaders of the Ranghars were the two peasants Bisarat Ali of Kharkhauda and Baher Khan of Rohtak. To help them, Emperor Bhadurshah also sent an army under the Command of Tafzal Husain. On 24th May, Loch, the

Deputy Commissioner of Rohtak, reached to control the situation, but in vain.

On 27th May the Haryana Light Infantry which was sent to crush the uprising at Hissar joined the people. Now, it was chaos and anarchy everywhere. The British Government tried to regain the power. They sent the 60th N.I. of Ambala from Panipat on 28th May under Loch, the D.C. of Rohtak. He reoccupied Rohtak but on 10th June his own army, the 5th N.I. revolted against him and the sepoys reached Delhi. The British authorities again made sternous efforts to occupy the district.

Consequently, Lieutenant W.S.R. Hodson, was sent with a big force on 15th August. At Kharkhauda, he met with a stiff resistance.[48] Anyhow, he reached Rohtak on 16th August. There was again a stiff fight on 17th August in which about 300 Ranghar horsemen under the leadership of Sahar Khan fought against him.[49] Anyhow, later on they left the field and Hodson returned to Delhi, leaving Sampla, Meham under the supervision of the Raja of Jind.

After sometime, in September, General Van Courtlandt, the Deputy Commissioner of Ferozepur was sent to Rohtak; Due to the fall of Delhi it was not difficult for him to maintain peace and order and to collect revenue.[50]

The people of Hissar, Hansi, and Sirsa also revolted. Their local leaders were Muhammed Azim, a descendant of the royal family of Delhi, Hukam Chand a jain businessman of Hansi, Nur Muhammad Khan of Rania and others.

At Hansi, on May 15, the 4th Irregular Cavalry revolted and reached Delhi. On May 27 the Haryana Light Infantry and the Dadri Cavalry revolted at Hissar. In this revolt, Wedderfurn, the Deputy Commissioner of Hissar, along with 12 other Europeans was killed. Then the rebels went to Hansi.

Similarly all prominent officials stationed at Sirsa like Captain Roberts, the Superintendent of Bhatiana, Donald, the Assistant Superintendent, Captain Hillard, Officer-Commanding of the Contingent, and others fled away and took shelter at Ferozepur and in Patiala State.

In the month of June efforts were made to control the District again. In the first week of June General Van Courtlandt, attacked the Hissar District. On 17th June Nur Samad Khan, the Nawab of

Rania, fought but was defeated and later arrested and hanged. General Van Courtlandt attacked the villages of Chatravan and Khaira. He reached Sirsa on 20th June and defeated the rebels[51] and re-established law and order. Courtlandt sent Captain Pearse[52] to Hissar who reached there on 26th June. He himself reached there on 17th July, and created a havoc among the people.[53] He looted the house of Prince Muhammad Azim and captured his Begum. Prince Muhammad Azim offered opposition but failed and he had to flee.

On 25th September the rebels went towards Tosham. They killed some of the Government officials and looted the treasury. On 26th September, they reached Hansi. But they were checked in the way of Courtlandt. Prince Muhammad Azim again fought but was unsuccessful.

In Panipat District, the people fought under the leadership of the Imam of the Shrine of Bu Ali Kalandhar but they were defeated and the Imam was arrested and hanged.[54] Some of the villages refused to pay land revenue. At Bullabh village, the jats under the leadership of Ram Lal opposed Captain Hughes of the 1st Punjab Cavalry, but later he suddenly attacked the village and suppressed the revolt.[55] Like Panipat, the people of Thanesar District revolted. In Karnal the people revolted but the British made security arrangements to control the G.T. Road with the help of the chiefs of the Jind and Karnal but the peasants of this area refused to pay land revenue.

At Thanesar town the people revolted with a beat of drum. When the D. C. Thanesar, Captain MacNiel heard the information, he disarmed a company of the rebel 5th N. I. on 14th July stationed at Thanesar. The British appealed to the chiefs of Patiala, Jind, Kunjpura and Karnal to help him. Consequently, the Maharaja of Patiala came to Thanesar from Jasomali, a village close to Ambala, with 1500 men and 4 guns on 15th May.[56] The chiefs of Jind, Kunjpura and Karnal also sent 400, 350, and 150 men respectively.[57] They guarded not only Thanesar, Karnal and Ambala, but also the G.T. Road from Karnal to Phillor.[58]

Similarly, the people of Ladwa, Pehowa, Pundri, Kaithal and Assandh also revolted. They refused to pay land revenue. Lieutenant Pearson and Captain MacNiel had a hard time in controlling Kaithal and Ladwa and Assandh[59] but later established their authority.

In Ambala, the 60th N. I. and the 5th N. I. revolted against the British but their revolt was suppressed. Later the 60th N. I. reached Rohtak, it revolted against the British. Similarly the 5th N. I. which was sent to Rupar under Captain Gardiner revolted under the leadership of Sardar Mohur Singh.[60] But anyhow, it was suppressed and Mohur Singh was hanged. There was disturbance at Jagadhri and the Maharaja of Patiala sent a force to help the British.[61]

To sum up, on the basis of the above evidences, it can be said that practically the whole of Haryana was in revolt by the end of May 1857.

The Impact

On the 16th of September 1857 Delhi fell. Bahadurshah with his wife Zinet Mahal and the family (two sons and a grandson) surrendered himself to Captain Hodson who shot the princes with his own hands,[62] and their dead bodies were thrown on the *chabutra*, near Kotwali. The King was also tried before the Martial Court and charged of aiding and abetting Muhammed Bakht Khan and his son Mirza Mughul in rebellion and proclaimed himself sovereign of India. He was also charged with committing the murder of 49 Europeans on 16th May.[63] He was found guilty of declaring war against the Queen and the massacre of British Residents. So he was sent to Rangoon with his family where he died on 7th September, 1862.

It is incorrect to say that at the time of the entry of the British army in Delhi again "no children or women and few, if any of the inhabitants, suffered at their hands."[64] In fact, during the following week Delhi witnessed a period of miseries, plunder, arson and rape.[65]

Great territorial changes were made. In fact, the principls of compensation and rewards to the helpers and the punishments and penalties to the opponents of the British was adopted. Except the three small states of Pataudi, Dujana, and Loharu, all the other important states like Jhajjar, Dadri, Farukhanagar, Ballabhgarh, Buria, Kalsia were confiscated. These were either merged with other states or were given to the loyal chiefs. Maharaja Narender Singh of Patiala who showed the greatest loyalty[66] and belped the British with 8 guns, 2156 horsçmen, 2846 infantry with 156 officers was rewarded[67] with the *parganas* of Narnaul valued at

₹ 2,00,000 a year, the supermacy over the Bhadour, the confiscated house of Zinet Mahal worth ₹ 10,000.[68] Maharaja Sarup Singh of Jind received the Dadri territory of 575 sq. miles of ₹ 1,03,000 per year, 13 villages[69] in the Kularan area of rental value of ₹ 13,810, the confiscated house of Prince Mirza Abu Bakar of ₹ 6000/—.[70] Similarly, Raja Bharpur Singh of Nabha was awarded the *paraganas* of Bawal and Kanti in the confiscated Jhajjar territory of ₹ 1,06,000 per year.[71] Later on 18th January 1860, when Lord Canning, the Viceroy of India visited Ambala held a *durbar* and confirmed all the above grants and certain other concessions were declared.[72] Most of the *jagirdars* in Haryana helped the British and consequently, they were rewarded for their loyalty.

While the loyalists were rewarded, the rebels were punished. Three of the prominent feudal chiefs of Haryana[73] were tried and hanged at the Kotwali in Chandni Chowk, Delhi, and their property was confiscated. They were Abdur Rehman of Jhajjar (23rd January 1858), Ahmed Ali of Farrukhanagar (23rd January 1858) and Nahar Singh of Ballabhgarh (9th January 1858). Bhadurjang Khan of Dadri was also tried and was deprived of his territory of ₹ 1,50,000. But he was given pension and removed to Lahore. In villages, many *chaudharies* and *lambardars* who helped the rebels were deprived of their land and property. Property rights of sonie villages were forfeited. In some villages heavy penalties were imposed. In Gurgaon and Hissar districts more than 368 people were hanged or transported for life imprisonment. In Rohtak a collective penalty of ₹ 63,000/- was imposed on the people of Rohtak. Especially the Ranghars, Shaikhs and Kesai the residents of Qila Mohalla became its victim.[74]

At Thanesar ₹ 2,35,000 and at Ambala ₹ 25,3591 were forcibly collected as fines.[75] In fact, the region as a whole guffered a grave set back. It was detached from the North-western provinces and tagged with Punjab in February 1858. Some of the districts and tehsils of the region were reorganised.[76] Under the administration of Sir John Lawrence, it had remained an eye-sore for the British officials. All progress was rendered impossible as the price of freedom struggle. For example, no canal was constructed, no new roads, except already accepted, planned, no educational institution set up. No industry, no trade and even no facilities for agriculture were provided. It became a place of frequent famine, epedemic and an open field for the Christian missionaries. The

British left the starving peasantry of Haryana with the only choice of joining the British armies in the vain hope of subduing the indomitable spirit which had long scorned their power.

NOTES

1. S.N. Sen: *Eighteen Fifty-seven*, p. 402.
2. S.C. Mittal: *Adhunik Bharat Ka Arthik Itihas* (Jullundur, 1976), pp. 10-11.
3. D.R. Gadgil: *The Industrial Evolution of India in Recent Times*, (Calcutta, 1950), p. 9.
4. *The Imperial Gazetteer of India*, Oxford, 1909 (Reprint, New Delhi, 1971) Vol. V, See *Karnal District*, pp. 55-57.
5. *Ibid.*, Vol. XIII See *Hissar District*, p. 153.
6. *Ibid.*
7. *Ibid.*
8. *Ibid*
9. *Ibid.*
10. *Ibid*, Vol. XI, p. 231.
11. For detail See *Settlement Report Karnal*, p. 47; *Seulement Report, Delhi*, p. 141.
12. R.M. Bird's *Memorandum on Land Revenue Settlement dated*, Feb. 22, 1842 vide, *Home Revenue Proceedings* Nos. 7-8 of August 21,1844. For detail see Dharm Bhanu: *History of Administration of the North-Western Provinces*, Agra, p. 173.
13. R.C. Dutta: *Economic History of India in the Victorian Age*, p. 35.
14. *R.M. Bird's Memorandum*, dated Feb- 22, 1842.
15. Secretary to N.W.P. *Govt.* to Board of Revenue, No. 2846, dated Dec. 31, 1842 vide, *Boord of Revenue Proceedings*, No. 34 of March 24, 1843. See Dharm Bhanu: *op. cit.*, p. 173.
16. Dharm Bhanu: *op. cit.*, p. 174.
17. *Bird's Memorandum of* Feb. 22, 1842.
18. 196 *patwaris* were dismissed in Delhi division in 1833.
19. James Thomason (1804-1853) joined the Judicial Branch of the Company, appointed Registrar in Sadr Adalat Court, Secretary to Government, appointed Collector and Magistrate of Azamgarh District in N.W. Provinces, did survey and settlement work there, Secretary to the Agra Government, Member of the Board of Revenue, Foreign Secretary to the Government of India, appointed the Lieutenant-Governor of the N.W.P. in 1843, died on Sept. 27, 1853. For detail see G D. Oswell : *Sketches of Rulers of India*, Vol. II, pp. 174-94 ; Richard Temple : *James Thomason*, (Rulers of India Series), Oxford; W. Muir: *James Thomason-Late Lieutenant-Governor*, (London, 1879).
20. *Calcutta Review*, Vol. XII, No . 23 July 1849.
21. Percival Spear: *Twilight of the Mughals*, pp. 105-6.
22. *Ibid.*
23. L.H. Griffith: *The Rajas of the Punjab*, p. 178; *The Imperial Gazetteer of India*, Vol. XIII, p. 153.
24. *The Imperial Gazetteer of India*, Vol. XI, p. 230.
25. R. Martin Montgomery: *The History of Indian Empire*, Vol. II, p. 9.

26. Bentinck's Minute on the affairs of Rajputana and Delhi, 30th March 1832 vide C.H. Phillip (Ed.); *The Correspondence of Lord William Cavendish Bentinck,* (1828-1835) 2 Vols. (Oxford, 1977), pp. 1483.
27. *Ibid.*
28. Dharm Bhanu: *op. cit.*, pp. 253-260 (for detail see pp. 221-260).
29. Buddha Prakash: *Glimpses of Haryana,* pp. 89-91.
30. *The Imperial Gazetteer of India,* Vol. XI, p. 227.
31. Quoted by K.C. Yadav: *The Revolt of 1857 in Haryana,* (New Delhi, 1977), p. 33.
32. *Ibid.*
33. *Ibid.*, pp. 55-96.
34. *Ibid.*, p. 49.
35. Percival Spear: *op. cit.*, p. 194.
36. *Ibid.*, p. 202.
37. *Ibid.*
38. For Delhi events see Percival Spear; *op. cit.*, pp. 202-217; R.C. Majumdar: *The Sepoy Mutiny and Revolt of 1857,* (Calcutta, 1963), pp. 81-83; Mahadi Husain: *Bahadur Shah II and the War of 1857 in Delhi,* (Delhi, 1958), pp. 156-281; S.B.H. Rizvi, *Swantra Delhi,* (Varansi, 1957), pp. 41-61; Dr. Prabha Chopra: *op. cit.*, pp. 61-75; Ramvilas Sharma; *Sunsatavana Ki Kranti,* (Agra, 1957), pp. 199- 276.
39. Buddha Prakash: *Haryana through the Ages,* p. 90.
40. *The Gurgaon District Gazetteer,* pp. 24-25.
41. Jwala Sahai: *Tarikh-i-Mewat,* pp. 258-259. Quoted by K.C. Yadav: *Revolt of 1857 in Haryana,* p. 58.
42. Percival Spear: *op. cit.*, p. 207; Shri Ram Sharma: *Haryana Ka Nau Rattan,* (Rohtak, 1978), p. 23.
43. K.C. Yadav: *Revolt of 1857 in Haryana,* p. 59; Sbri Ram Sharma: *Haryana Ke Nau Rattan,* p. 23.
44. K.C. Yadav: *Revolt of 1857 in Haryana,* p. 113.
45. *Ibid.*, p. 117; See also Lt. Col. G.B. Malleson; *The Red* Pamphlet (*The Mutiny of the Bengal Army*), (London, 1858), p. 319.
46. *Ibid.*, p. 120.
47. C.J. Griffiths: *Siege of Delhi,* (London, 1910), pp. 96-7.
48. Buddha Prakash: *Haryana through the Ages,* p. 90.
49. J. Cave-Brown: *The Punjab and Delhi in 1857,* Vol. II, (Edinburgb, 1861), pp. 146-47.
50. J.W. Kaye: *A History of the Sepoy War in India,* (1857-63), Vol. II. (London, 1878), p. 107.
51. Marx & Engels: *The First Indian War of Independence,* (1857-59), (Moscow, fourth edition, 1975), p. 58. (Originally an article entitled, 'The Indian Insurrection' by K. Marx on August 14, 1857 published in the New York, Daily Tribune, No. 5104, of August 29, 1857).
52. For the detail of Captain Pearse activities in Hissar District. See Frederic Cooper: *Crisis in Punjab,* pp. 8-10.
53. Marx and Engels: *op. cit.*, p. 74 (Originally an article entitled 'The Revolt in India'by Karl Marx on Sept. 1, 1857, Published in New York. Daily Tribune, No. 5118, of Sept. 15, 1857.

54. *The Karnal District Gazetteer*, p. 40.
55. J. Cave-Brown: *op. cit.*, Vol. II, p. 143.
56. According to L.H. Griffin the number of troops were 1300. *The Rajas of the Punjab*, p. 234.
57. *Punjab Govt. Records* Vol. VIII-I, pp. 27-28.
58. L.H. Griffin: *The Rajas o f the Punjab*, p. 235.
59. Buddha Prakash: *Haryana through the Ages*, p. 90.
60. *Ibid.*, p. 91; *Punjab Govt. Records*, Vol. VIII-I, p. 37.
61. L.H. Griffin: *The Rajas of the Punjab*, p. 236.
62. Marx & Engels: *op. cit*. p. 174.
63. Percival Spear: *op. cit.*, pp. 222-23.
64. Syed Muhammed Latif: *History of the Punjab*, p. 581.
65. Maulvi Sayyid Ahmad Ali: *Yadgar i-Delhi*, (1903) Quoted by Teja Singh: *History of the Haryana*, (New Delhi, 1974), p. 109.
66. L.H. Griffin: *The Rajas of the Punjab*, p. 233.
67. *Ibid.*, p. 236; Buddha Prakash: *Haryana through the Ages*, p. 93.
68. L.H. Griffin: *The Rajas of the Punjab*, pp. 236-39.
69. The thirteen villages were Bhaiapura, Alampur, Balampur, Kularan, Dodura, Rotli, Rangoli, Dharmgarh, Buzuig, Saipura, Mani, Kalkagarh and Shahpur.
70. L.H. Griffin: *The Rajas of the Punjab*, pp. 393-94.
71. *Ibid.*, p. 466.
72. *Ibid.*, pp. 254-57.
73. For the role of the feudal chiefs in Haryana see K.C. Yadav: *The Revolt of 1857 in Haryana*, pp. 81-107.
74. Shri Ram Sharma: *Haryana Ka Itihas*, pp. 38, 41.
75. V.N. Datta and H.A. Phadke; *History of the Kurukshetra*, p. 212.
76. Shri Ram Sharma: *Haryana Ka Itihas*, pp. 44-47.

4

Socio-Religious Awakening in Haryana

The later half of the 19th century was a period of social and religious awakening and the growth of a new spirit leading to socio-religious movements, These movements, with regional differences, were more or less identical in character, because the focus was on the socio-economic and religious uplift of the society. These movements produced a multifarious intellectual expression of the social and cultural transformations.[1] In majority of the cases religion was the basic guiding source.[2]

In Haryana also, some movements sprang up among the Muslim and the Hindu communities. Their main objects were the eradication of social evils, the education of the people and the revival of their old religion.

In order to know the popular awakening in the different spheres, it would be pertinent to have a graphic account of the socio-religious movements, the development of the education and literacy and the growth of the literature and the press.

The Wahabi Movement

One of the movements which presented a serious challenge to the British authority[3] was the Wahabi movement. Originally started in Arbia by Muhammad Ibn Abdul Wahab[4] (1707-1787), got its inspiration from Imam Ibn Taimiya of the Hanbali, a school of Muslim theology. The movement was 'primarily a religious'[5] or puritan Islamic.[6] In fact, it was a Muslim revivalist movement. Its main object in the beginning was the abolition of tribalism in Arabia.[7]

In India the leader of the movement was Syed Ahmad (1786-1831) of Rae Bareli, now a district of U.P. He tried to bring revival in Muslim community by means of threefold activities, "the exalation of the word of God, the revival of the spirit of faith in word and deed, and the practice of holy war."[8] He toured a number of towns and cities where his activities were highly admired. Before starting the *Jehad* or Holy war, he made a journey to Mecca in 1822. After his return in 1824 he founded "a system by which they (his followers) affected one of the greatest revivals known to Indian History, and which has kept alive the spirit of revolt against the British rule during fifty years."[9]

Syed Ahmad designed himself *Imam Mahadi, Imam-Humam, Amir-ul-Musliman* and *Khalifa*. The North-West Frontier was selected as the base of operations. He raised a strong group of fighters. A number of pamphlets were written. Military training was given to its volunteers. In the social and economic fields, he helped the poor peasant to resist tyranny and oppression.

The Wahabis in India launched a movement for the overthrow of the Sikh kingdom in Punjab and the British from India. Syed Ahmad established himself in the Swat Valley where he waged a *Jehad* against the Sikhs. But in the pitched battle of Balakot (a village in the Kunhar Pass) in 1831 he lost his life.[10] Syed Ahmad's sudden death did not subside the enthusiasm. In fact, he had already created a well-knit organisation from Decca to Peshawar[11] and established his centres in all the important towns of the country. The headquarters of the movement was at Patna.[12] Agents were appointed for the collection of funds and the recruitment of volunteers.

The death of Ranjit Singh and the first Anglo-Sikh War (1845-46) made the British paramount in the Punjab. Now the movement soon assuming a political and military character against the British. The British also started operations against them through the Special Police Department and by the armed expeditions on the Frontier. Between 1850 and 1863 nearly twenty expeditions were sent in which 60,000 troops were sent against the Wahabis.[13] When the military operations failed, the campaign of police action, followed by judicial prosecutions was speeded up.[14]

During these state-trials, a number of centres for the efficient working of the anti-British movement came to notice. Robert

Montgomery, Judicial Commissioner of the Punjab, reported that the Muslims of Patna and Thanesar were in correspondance with the 64th N.I. near Peshawar and urged it to revolt.[14a] Haryana region was one of the major centres of its activities. Some of the disgruntled Muslim *zamindars* joined it.[15] Besides Delhi, some of its important centres were Thanesar, Ambala, Pehowa and Panipat.

Some of the notable leaders of Haryana were Maulvi Muhammad Qasim of Panipat, Husaini of Thanesar, Muhammed Jafar of Thanesar and Muhammed Shafi of Ambala, a contracter for the supply of meat to Europeans in all the cantonments from Ambala to Naushera.[16] Muhammed Qasim was one of the closest associates of Syed Ahmad. He went to Sithana, the headquarters of the North-west Frontier and worked with the tribal chief Syed Akbar Shah. He also wrote inspiring letters to Maulvis Wilayat Ali and Inayat Ali, the leaders of the Patna Centre.[17] Muhammad Jafar alias Peeroo Khan, was a disciple of Wilayat Ali of Patna.[18] He was the incharge of the north-western region of India. In fact, he was the nucleus of all the activities of Wahabi Movement in Haryana. Thanesar was described by the British "as one of the main depots"[19] and Jafar as "one of its Chief Organisers." Though born in a poor family, simply a petition writer, in 1856 became a *lambardar* of Thanesar, but he considerably helped the Wahabis in fighting the British authority.[20]

In 1863-64 the net-work of the organisation was exposed due to one Ghuzzan Khan,[21] a Pathan police Sergeant at *Chowki* Panipat, Karnal District. Soon Muhammed Jafar and others were arrested. In the state-trial at Ambala before Sir Herbert Edwards, the Commissioner of Ambala,[22] in 1864, the activities of the Wahabis came into light. Some of the leaders were condemned to long sentences of imprisonment, others sent to the Andaman Islands. With the arrest of Muhammad Jafar, the movement virtually "met its doom" after 1864.[23] It was completely suppressed in India by 1888.

Though the movement failed yet it left its impact. Probably this was the first planned and highly organised revolutionary movement after the uprising of 1857.[24] But being a purely Muslim movement for the revival of their community and for establishing the Muslim rule in India against the English as well as other 'infidels', it could not be appreciated by the other communities. In fact, it gave an impetus to separatist tendencies in Indian society and widened the gulf between the Hindus and the Muslims.[25] Secondly, the movement, gave a turn to the politics which came to be dominated by religious dogmas.[26] It also kept alive the desire for freedom among the Muslims.[27]

The Arya Samaj

Like the Wahabi Movement, the Arya Samaj was revivalist in form and reformist in content.[28] It exercised a profound influence in Haryana. Originally launched in the second half of the 19th century,[29] it became popular among the Hindus,[30] particularly young men.[31] According to the official view it was a Hindu reformed church representing the reaction of Hinduism against the Christian religion, Western science and Western domination.[32]

Swami Dayanand, its founder, got a fertile land for his ideology not at his birthplace at Tankara (now in Gujarat State), but in the towns of Punjab and in the rural areas of Haryana. After establishing the Arya Samaj on April 10, 1875 at Bombay, Dayanand proceeded northwards and visited Delhi to attend the *Durbar* in January 1877. He thought that his visit to Delhi would provide a good opportunity of propagating Vedic religion.[33] At Delhi he was invited by some of the prominent leaders of the Punjab. Consequently he accepted the proposal and made his first visit to Ludhiani on 31st March 1877. The first Samaj in Punjab was established at Lahore on 24th June 1877. He toured the prominent places of the Punjab. In his speeches he attacked idolatory, child-marriage and propagated the re-marriage of widows and the female education. While he praised Vedas as a source of eternal knowledge, he vehementally criticised Christianity and the activities of their missionaries. He also preached that the Vedas inculcated monotheism and attacked Hinduism which is based upon the Purans. He accepted *Shastras* as the main tool of proselytization.

The first place of Haryana visited by Swami Dayanand was Ambala.[34] On 17th July 1878 he halted for sometimes while going from Punjab to Roorkee in U.P. Here he condemned the social and religious weaknesses of the orthodox Hinduism. In 1880 Swami Dayanand visited Rewari at the request of Rao Yudhister,[35] the

Ahir leader and the descendent of Rao Tula Ram. Later he became the disciple of Swami Dayanand. Swami Dayanand delivered eleven religious discourses,[36] and took part in discussions. He again made violent attack on Puranic gossips, incarnatism etc. At this appeal of Swami Dayanand a *Goshala* was established at Rewari. Perhaps, it was the first *Goshala* in Northern India.[37]

After the death of Swami Dayanand on 30th October 1883, the Arya Samaj soon became popular in Haryana by the efforts of Lala Lajpat Rai, Pandit Basti Ram, Lala Chandu Lal, Dr. Ramji Das and Rao Yudhister and his family members. In 1883, its branches were established at Rohtak and Karnal. In Karnal it was established on 7th October by Swami Atmananda. In 1886 Jagadhri Arya Samaj was started by Pandit Lekh Raj of Punjab. In 1890 at Rewari, the Arya Samaj was established by the efforts of Rao Yudhister. In 1891, the Ambala Cantonment Arya Samaj was established under the presidentship of Sardar Kala Singh. In nutshell, all the prominent Arya Samajs in Haryana like the Arya Samajs at Panipat, Rohtak, Hissar, Narnodh (Hissar), Milakhpur (Hissar), Sinkpathry (Karnal), Jind etc. were established during the 1890's.

Perhaps in Haryana the expansion of Arya Samaj was on more sound footing than elsewhere even in Punjab.[38] In Haryana, Hinduism, being surrounded and infilitrated by the Islam and Sikh faith, was not as rigid as it was elsewhere.[39] The caste system was less rigid in comparison to other parts of the country. The Brahmans were unable to dominate large and powerful groups like the Jats.[40] The Brahmins were also not so rigid. Perhaps, it was due to the absence of big towns and cities in Haryana that the rural masses had easily been attracted by the philosophy of Dayanand. The Arya Samaj made strenuous efforts to raise the social status of the lower communities.

Being agriculturaly dominated region, 'story of Jat' in Satyarth Prakash (Chapter XI) appealed them very much. Dayanand's appeal for the protection of cow and encouragement to eat vegetables touched their heart. Dayanand also provided them a weapon against the Christianity. Similarly, it was due to the energetic leadership that it gained a stable positon in Haryana. Lala Lajpat Rai made it popular during his short stay at Hissar.

Pandit Basti Ram[41] played a dynamic role in this respect. His *Bhajan* and other works like *Pakhand Khandni* and *Aughmurshan Prathana* became very popular. Later, in the early twentieth century, Swami Brahmananda, Bhagat Phul Singh, Pandit Lakhpat Rai (Hissar) and Lala Chuda Mani pleader (Hissar) were its notable leaders.[42]

During the first decade of the twentieth century, the branches of the Arya Samaj were also established at Radaur, Bamla, Disaur, Khari, Farmana, Salwan, Thol, Kalka, Gurgaon and Sohna. Like the Arya Samajs in Punjab, it was also divided into College Party and Gurukul Party, while the centre of the former was Hissar and Karnal Districts, the later dominated in Rohtak District.

In fact, with the beginning of the twentieth century, the Arya Samaj emerged as a vital force. Besides the religious activities it centred its programmes in eradication of social evils and helping the poor and propagating the educational activities.

The Arya Samaj denounced caste rigidity and advocated the freedom of movement from one caste to another based on *Gun* (character) *Karam* (action) and *Swabhava* (nature).[43]

It also made efforts to raise the status of the untouchables. It took interest in the social uplift of the lower and oppressed classes. According to them, it was mainly due to bad environment, association, and training resulting deterioration of character.[44] Later, it started a *Shudhi* movement to prevent low caste Hindus from embracing Christianity or Islam and to purify them for their inclusion in Hinduism.

The Arya Samajis campaigned against the social evils. They launched a fiery crusade against infant-marriage. They supported the consent Bill of 1891 which extended the age of the girls for the marriage. They advocated widow-marriage. According to the Deputy Commissioner Gurgaon: "This is the only religious movement which has spread during the last ten years .... One great resuit of its spread has been the diminution in expenditure of marriages and other occasion which is a move in the right direction."[45] The Arya Samaj was perhaps the first purely Indian association to organise orphans and widow homes.[46] The first orphanage was established in Punjab at Ferozepur in 1877, during the time of Dayanand.[47] A significant work in this regard was done by the Hissar Arya Samaj and the Bhiwani Hindu Orphanage under the leadership of Lala Chandu Lal and Lala Chudamani, the President and the Secretary, respectively.

Besides the religious and social sphere, in education also, some efforts were made by the Arya Samaj. The 'Gurukul System' of the Arya Samaj attracted the people of Haryana. The first *Gurukul* was established at Gujranwala in Punjab on 16th May 1900, which was transferred to Kangri (Haridwar) on 4th March 1902.[48] In 1911, the first Gurukul in Haryana was established at Kurukshetra. It was established with the help of Lala Jyoti Prasad of Thanesar who contributed the land and a cash amount of ₹ 10,000.[49] Its foundation stone was laid by Swami Shardhananda.[50] Later *Gurukuls* were established at Rohtak in Matindu (1915), Bhanswal (1918), Jhajjar (1924). As regards the female education Arya Samaj Hissar gave the lead. A number of Kanya Pathshalas were opened at different places in Haryana.

Unlike education, it was the national activities which upset the British Government. In 1900 Congress Session at Lahore for the first time nearly over one hundred Arya Samajis were present and several of them made speeches. Perhaps the Government could not tolerate the popularity of the Arya Samaj. The years between 1906 and 1910 were rather critical for the Arya Samaj.[51] The C.I.D. reports from 1907 to 1910 are replete with news about the Arya Samaj. To the British Government, the Arya Samaj was the 'greatest enemy' of the Government and the 'most dangerous anti-British movement'.[52] According to the official view, the Arya Samaj was mainly responsible for sedition. In 1907 Sir Denzil Ibbeston, the Lieutenant-Governor of Punjab stated that he had been informed by nearly every District Magistrate of Punjab that wherever there was Arya Samaj, it was the centre of seditious talk.[53] Later Sir Michael O'Dwyer, the Lieutenant-Governor of Punjab also expressed the similar view.[54]

Like Punjab, in Haryana also a "fairly large number of Arya Samajis were shadowed by the C.I.D. men."[55] They were suspected when they wanted to enlist themselves in the Indian Army.[56] The members of the Arya Samaj were branded as "wicked, unscrupulous person". Thier literature was confiscated and their flag torn up.[57] In Panipat, on the Diaries of three *zamindars*, it was mentioned, "*Zaildar* is good but he is Arya Samaji. So an eye should be kept on him."[58] The Deputy Commissioner Karnal instigated people to make fictitious case on the persons who were Arya Samajis.[59] The Seditious Meetings Act was employed for curbing the Arya Samaj activities in Rohtak and Hissar.[60] In fact, they played a significant role in the national movement, which will be studied later.

In short, it can be said that it was both social and national movement.[61] Social and educational activities of the Arya Samaj through lectures, meetings, and pamphlets contributed to create the climate of public opinion. It encouraged the reading of the Vedas and attacked Purans and orthodox Hinduism. It created a feeling of self-reliance, faith and patriotism among the youth and in a way it had a big impact on the Indian mind and prepared the ground for nationalism.

The Sanatan Dharma Sabha

Like the Arya Samaj, the other society of note was Sanatan Dharma Sabha, which was founded by Pandit Din Dayalu Sharma[62] of Jhajjar. In 1886 it was first established at Jhajjar and then spread out in the various parts of the province. Its chief objects[63] were the reformation and preaching of the Sanatan Dharma, the eradication of the prevailing social evils, the encouragement of the Sanskrit and Hindi languages, the opening of the educational institutions and inculcating an urge for social service. Its basic aspects were the respect for gods and goddesses and faith in the theory of incarnation. Perhaps, it would be incorrect to say that its origin took place as a reaction to the Arya Samaj.

To fulfil its mission, a number of its branches were established at prominent towns and cities of Haryana like Bhiwani, Hissar, Sirsa, Karnal, Kurukshetra, Safidon, Rewari, Palwal, Kaithal, Rohtak, Beri and Gurgaon.

As early as in 1886, after attending the second Congress Session at Calcutta, Pandit Din Dayalu Sharma planned to organise an all India religious conference on the pattern of the Congress.[64] Consequently, at Haridwar he founded the *Bharat Dharma Mahamandal*, the main body of the society. In its inaugural session several prominent religious leaders like Colonel Alcot of Theosophical Society, Raja Harbans Lal of Sheikhupura, Diwan Ramjas of Kapurthalas, Bal Mukand Gupta and Pandit Ambika Dutt Vyas delivered lectures.[65] Soon it became all India Society. Its sessions were held at Haridwar, Mathura and Lahore.

The Sanatan Dharma Sabha became popular movement in Haryana during the last decade of the 19th century. Some of its notable local leaders were Nathu Lal, Pandit Chander Bhan, Pandit Harbanslal Sharma of Jhajjar ; Lala Sohan Lal and Hargolal Sharma of Hissar. Similarly some of the other prominent leaders were Lala Ganda Ram of Ambala Cantt, Pandit Harihar Swarup Sharma, Pandit Mauli Chander Sharma, the son of Pandit Din Dayalu Sharma, Goswami Ganesh Dutta and Pandit Neki Ram Sharma of Bhiwani.

Some of its leaders made extensive tours of the country. A number of religious discourses were given at various places. A Krishan Mandir was established at Simla by the efforts of Pandit Din Dayalu Sharma.

In educational sphere, a number of Sanatan Dharma Schools and later colleges were established. Din Dayalu Sharma helped in establishing some of the privately managed institutions like Hindu College at Delhi, Sanatan Dharma College at Lahore (now at Ambala), Visudhananda Vidyalaya at Calcutta and Marwar Vidyalaya at Bombay.

The Sanatan Dharma Sabha also propagated the study of Sanskrit and Hindi. Some Sanskrit *pathshalas* were also established. People were advised to use Hindi in courts. It encouraged the establishments of the libraries and reading rooms.

Like education and language, in social sphere also, some efforts were made to eradicate the social evils. They attacked the use of tobacco and liquor, the child-marriage, the extravagencce on litigation etc. They opposed the dancing of the prostitutes at marriages. Some orphanages were also established by the Sanatan Dharma Sabha. They also advocated widow-remarriage and removal of the untouchability.

To sum up, it can be said that the Sanatan Dharma Sabha also, though to a lesser extent, helped in the reconstruction of the Hindu society in Haryana. On the whole while the Arya Samaj was more popular in Haryana, the Sanatan Dharma Sabha was more popular outside Haryana.

Development of Education and Literacy

Educationally, Haryana was one of the most backward regions of India. In the sphere of education and literacy it always got the step-motherly treatment during the British regime. Neither the British authority nor the private agencies paid any serious attention to its progress.

Though the British occupied the Haryana region earlier than the Punjab itself, no progress was made even in the Indigenous education. The following table gives66 the progress of Indigenous education in Haryana including Delhi in 1882.

The table on next page shows the various types of Indigenous schools. The Maktabs and Madrasas, the Sanskrit and Nagri Pathshalas, the Gurmuki schools represented Muslims, Hindus and Sikhs institutions respectively.[67] Their main object was the preaching of religious instructions, while the Mahajani schools fulfilled the need of the trading classes. In the whole of Punjab,[68] while there were 13,109 indigenous schools with 1,33,588 pupils, in Haryana region, there were only 773 schools with 10,404 pupils.

As regards the growth of the western education, it was very low. Perhaps, Fraser, an Assistant was the first British Officer who established four schools in the *pargana* of Sonepat during 1816 to 1823.[69] But after sometime, due to paucity of funds these schools were closed.[70] In fact, nothing was done upto 1840's. With the proposal of a grant-in-aid System by the Wood's despatch in 1854 some Tehsildari' schools were established in the districts of Delhi, Gurgaon and Rohtak in 1856, and in the remaining districts after sometime. These schools were of middle standard and their medium of instruction was either Hindi or Urdu or both.

Some of the Middle and High schools were also established. These schools were established at Shahabad, Ladwa, Thanesar, Kaithal, Sadhora and Ropar in Ambala district; Sonepat and Nazafgarh in Delhi; Panipat in Karnal; Hansi in Hissar; Gurgaon and Palwal in Gurgaon, and Jhajjar and Bahadurgarh in Rohtak.[71] High schools were also established at important towns like Karnal, Rohtak, Bhiwani, Reweri, Delhi and Jagadhari.[72]

In fact, some development in education in Haryana was made after 1870. For instance in 1900-1901 Ambala District had 180 schools with 9,133 pupils, Karnal District 203 with 5,373 pupils, Rohtak District 98 with 5,097 pupils, Hissar District 105 with 5,085 pupils and Gurgaon district 128 with 5, 139 pupils.

Progress of Indigenous Education in Haryana (Including Delhi) in 1882

District	*No. of Maktabs and Madrasas*	*No. of Pupils*	*No. of Sanskrit and Nagri schools*	*No. of Pupils*	*No. of Gurumukhi schools*	*No. of Pupils*	*No. of Hindi Mahajani schools*	*No. of Pupils*	*Total No. of indigenous schools*	*Total No. of pupils*
Delhi	141	2073	19	177	—	—	56	1054	216	3304
Karnal	43	538	11	111	1	8	22	385	77	1042
Hissar	46	592	12	133	—	—	8	386	66	1111
Rohtak	45	452	33	351	—	—	21	381	99	1184
Sirsa	101	763	5	23	10	55	6	173	122	1014
Ambala	82	1018	19	303	7	66	30	703	138	2090
Gurgaon	24	236	6	65	—	—	25	358	55	659
Total	482	5672	105	1163	18	129	168	3440	773	10404

As regards the extent of literacy, it was very low. The influence of western education was not so intense here as in other provinces like Madras, Bombay and Bengal. However Delhi District occupied the highest percentage of literacy in the Haryana region *i.e.* 4.6% while Ambala District cames next with 4.3% literacy. The rate of progress of other four districts was very low as the following table shows:[73]

Literacy in 1900-1901

District	*Total %*	*% Males*	*% Females*
Delhi	4.6	8	0.6
Ambala	4.3	7.5	0.4
Karnal	2.4	4.3	0.1
Hissar	2.7	5.0	0.1
Rohtak	2.7	5.0	0.1
Gurgaon	—	—	—

The various district gazetteers indicate that Delhi was the 5th of 28 districts in respect of the literacy of its population, while Hissar District was 25th of 28 districts of the Punjab. The reasons for its educational backwardness was poverty of the peasants, expensive education, lack of interest, lapse of the government, and the little interest shown by other agencies or individuals.[74] In fact, the education was not valued by the masses.[75]

As regards the female education, the progress was far from satisfactory. The highest literacy among women were in Delhi District which was only 0.6%. In fact, despite efforts on the part of the government and other agencies no progress was made.

As regards higher education in and adjoining Haryana region, the only institution until 1877 was the Delhi College, founded in 1792 supported by the voluntary contributions and later aided by the government. In 1828 in it teaching of English was started. In 1877 it was removed to Lahore and merged with the Lahore Government College. In 1882 St. Stephen Mission College (which was originally started in 1864 and later merged with the Delhi College) was restarted. In 1890 Hindu College was started at Delhi by the efforts of the Sanatan Dharma Sabha.

Besides there were two normal schools *i.e.* Teachers Training Schools at Ambala and at Delhi (1860) and the former was merged in Delhi College in 1864. So it can be concluded in true sense that up to the beginning of the twentieth century, except a few High schools at various places in Haryana, there was not a single college or training schools except at Delhi.

Even the total expenditure on education was very low. For instance, the expenditure incurred on education in 1901-2 was as below:

Ambala district	₹ 72,615
Karnal district	₹ 53,650
Hissar district	₹ 44,863
Rohtak district	₹ 44,047
Gurgaon district	₹ 46,836

To sum up, it can be said that the slow development in education greatly affected the progress of the region in various fields. It deprived the people from the contact with the Western education, culture and literature. Unlike other provinces, in Haryana one does not find the emergence of the English educated middle class up to the close of the 19th century. Infact Haryana remained deprived of the progress in the social, religious and political fields. Perhaps this was the main cause of late political awakening in Haryana.

Crowth of Literature and the Press

Like education, the increase in the production of literary Works and periodicals in Haryana up to the beginning of the twentieth century was very slow. Some of the notable writers were Balmukand Gupta, Madhva Prasad Misra, Bishamber Nath Sharma, Tulsi Ram Denesh and Pandit Basti Ram. Their works aroused the feeling of patriotism, self-reliance among the masses and high-lighted the evils prevailing in the society.

In the sphere of press the progress was very little. In fact the press was yet to be developed. Even up to the first two decades of the twentieth century there were only a few newspapers. Mostly the periodicals were Urdu weeklies and monthlies. Some of the notable papers[77] were *Sadiq-ul-Akhar*, a religious organ from Rewari, *Jyotish Martand*, an astrological paper from Gurgaon. Some papers represented their caste bias,[78] for example, *Ahir Patrika* from Rewari, *Jat Gazette* and *Jat Sepoy* from Rohtak, *Thakur Patrika* from Hissar, and *Brahmin Samachar* from Jagadhri. The *Cantonment Advocate* of Ambala generally represented the grievances of the people of Ambala.[79] There was another paper *Bharat Pratap* in Urdu from Jhajjar whose editor was Pandit Bishambar Dayal Sharma.80

In fact, in Haryana there was hardly an y newspaper with a political fevour. So it can be said that education, literature and the press—instruments of social and political change—were on a very low level.

NOTES

1. Charles H. Heimsath: *Indian Nationalism and Hindu Social Reform,* (Princeton, 1964), p. 3.
2. V.A. Narain: *Social History of Modern India: Nineteenth Century,* (Meerut, 1972), p. V.
3. Tara Chand: *History of the Freedom Movement in India,* Vol. II, (Delhi, 1967), p. 23.
4. L.S.S.O., Malley (Ed.): *Modern India and the West,* (Oxford, 1968), p. 369; R.C. Majumdar: *History of the Freedom Movement in India,* Vol. I, (Calcutta, 1971), p. 117.
5. A.J. Allen & Others: *The Cambridge Shorter History of India,* (Delhi, 1958), p. 717.
6. J.C. Powell-Price: *A History of India,* (New York, 1958), p. 545; L.S S.O. 'Malley: *op. cit.,* p. 395.
7. L.S.S.O. 'Malley: *op. cit.,* p. 396.
8. Tara Chand: *op. cit.,* Vol. Il, p. 23.
9. W.W. Hunter: *The Indian Musalmans,* (Third ed., Calcutta, 1876), pp. 61-62; *See also* Q. Ahmad: *The Wahabi Movement in India,* (Calcutta, 1966), p. 18.
10. V.A. Smith; *The Oxford History of India,* (Oxford, 1957), p. 802; Tara Chand: *op. cit.,* Vol. II, p. 26; For details see Q. Ahmad: *op. cit.,* pp. 63-98.
11. *Selections from the Records of the Govt. of Bengal Paper No. XLII,* pp. 72, 103, 130, 132, 134 quoted by S.B. Chaudhry: *Civil Disturbances During the British Rule in India 1765-1857,* (Calcutta, 1955), p. 51.
12. Briton Martin: *New India 1885,* (Oxford, 1970), p. 160.
13. R.C. Majumdar: *History of the Fteedom Movement in India,* Vol. I, p. 251; Tara Chand: *op. cit.,* p. 28.
14. Tara Chand: *op. cit.,* p. 28.

14(a). Salahuddin Malik: The Punjab and the Indian Mutiny, *Journal of Indian History,* Vol. I, Pt. II, (August 1972), 149, p. 346.

15. S. A. A. Rizvi: *Ideological Background of Wahabi Movement in India* in the XVIIIth and XIXth Century, *Ideas in History,* (Ed. by Bishashar Prasad), (Delhi, 1968), pp. 93-109.
16. Syed Muhammed Latif: *op. cit.,* p. 586.
17. Tara Chand: *op. cit.,* p. 27.
18. *Ibid.*
19. For detail see W.W. Hunter: *op. cit.,;* Q. Ahmad: *op. cit.,* p. 233.
20. V.N. Datta and H.A. Phadke: *History of the Kurukshetra,* (Kuruk- shetra, 1979), p. 215.

21. Q. Ahmad: *op. cit.*, p. 233.
22. Syed Muhammed Latif: *op, cit.*, p. 587.
23. B.K. Muztar : *Kurukshetra: Political and Cultural History*, p. 97.
24. R.C. Mujumdar: *History of the Fredom Movement in India*, Vol. I, pp. 251-52.
25. Tara Chand: *op. cit.*, Vol. II, p. 30.
26. *Ibid.*
27. *Ibid.*
28. P. Karunakaran: *Religion and Political Awakening in India*, (Meerut,. 1965), p. 2.
29. J. Nehru: *Discovcry of India*, (Calcutta, 1946), p. 235.
30. Ramsay MacDonald: *The Government of India*, London, 1919), p. 236; K.T. Paul; *The British Connection with India*, (London, 1926), p. 46; Valentine Chirol: *India* (London, 1926), p. 95; S.R. Sharma:

    The Arya Samaj and its impact on India in the 19th Century vide, *Ideas in History*, (Ed. by Bishashar Prasad), p. 157.
31. *Punjab Census Report, 1901*, p. 116.
32. *Home Department (political—B), Government of India*, Proceedings, July, 1911, Nos. 55-58.
33. H.B. Sharda: *Life of Dayanand Saraswati*, (Ajmer, 1946), p. 161.
34. R.C. Javed: *Punjab Ka Arya Samaj*, (Jullundur, 1964), p. 1.
35. Ranjit Singh: *Haryana Ka Arya Samaf Ka Itihas*, (Rohtak, Vikrami 2033), p. 8.
36. *Ibid.*, p. 9.
37. *Ibid.*
38. *Ibid.*, pp. 12-16.
39. L.S.S.O'Malley: *op. eit.*, p. 371.
40. Prem Chand: *The Social Reform Movement in Punjab*, (1873-1900), (Unpublished M, Phil. Thesis, Kurukshetra University, 1978), p. 53.
41. Padma Singh Sharma, 'Kamlesh': Pandit Basti Ram Kee Kavya Kala vide, *Journal of Haryana Studies*, Vol. I, No. 1, (Jan. 1969), pp. 93-96; Shri Ram Sharma: *Haryana Ka Itihas*, p. 49.
42. Shri Ram Sharma, *Haryana Ka Itihas*, p. 49.
43. G.P. Upadhaya: *The origin: Scope and Mission of the Arya Samaj*, (Allahabad, 1954), p. 9.
44. D.P. Pandey: *The Arya Samaj and Indian Nationalism*, (1875-1920), (New Delhi, 1972), p. 76.
45. *Punjab Census Report*, 1901, p. 116.
46. Lajpat Rai: *The Arya Samaj*, p. 125.
47. G.P. Upadhaya: *op. cit*, p. 117.
48. *Gurukul Kangri Ke Sath Varsha*, (Gurukul Kangri University, Haridwar, 1960), p. 9.
49. Balwan Singh Sulankhi: *Swami Sharadhanand*, (Unpublished M. Phil. Thesis, Kurukshetra University, 1978), p. 50.
50. *Ibid.*, p. 50; *Home Department (Political—B), Govt. of India*, Proceedings, March 1911, Nos. 1-4.
51. Lajpat Rai: *The Arya Samaj*, pp. 176-77.
52. *Home Department* (Political-Deposit), *Govt. of India*, Proceedings, April, 1912, No. 4.

53. *Home Department (Political—A), Govt. of India, Proceedings, August 1907, Nos. 148-235 ; The Panjabee,* 22-6-1907. 21-6-1907, and 16-10-1909.
54. Sir Michael O'Dwyer: *India as I knew it (1885-1925)*, London, 1925), p. 184.
55. Lajpat Rai: *The Arya Samaj,* pp. 176-77.
56. *Home Department (Political-Deposit), Govt. of India, Proceedings, August* 1910, No. 7.
57. S.S. Vidyalankar: *Jiwan Sangarsh,* (Delhi, 1964), p. 67; Ranjit Singh: *op. cit.*, pp. 27-28.
58. Ranjit Singh: *op. cit.*, p. 26.
59. *Ibid.*, pp. 26-27.
60. *Ibid.*, p. 30.
61. S.B. Choudhry: *Growth of Nationalism in India,* (New Delhi, 1973), p. 493.
62. *Pandit Din Dayalu Sharma Satabdi Granth,* p. 24.
63. *Punjab Census Report,* 1901, p. 115.
64. Dharm Vir Malik: Haryana Men Sanatan Dharm Sabha Ka Pursar, *Journal of Haryana Studies,* Vol. IX, Nos. 1-2 (1977), p. 54; Shri Ram Sharma: *Mere Apni Ram Kahani,* p. 4, Shri Ram Sharma: *Haryana Ke Nau Ratan,* pp. 30-31.
65. *Pandit Din Dayalu Sharma Sanshift Jiwan Charit,* p. 5.
66. The above table is based on G.W, Leitner's book *History of Indigenons Education in the Punjab since Annexation and in 1882,* (Reprint, 1971, Patiala), see Part II, pp. 1-32.
67. H.R. Mehta: *A History of the Growth and Development of Western Education in Punjab 1846-1884,* (Punjab Govt. Records Monographs No. 5, (First ed. 1929, Reprint, Patiala, 1971), pp. 14-15.
68. *Ibid.*, p. 19.
69. Sharp: *Selections from Educational Records,* (Delhi, 1965), Vol. I, pp. 13-15.
70. *Ibid.*
71. *The Punjab Education Reports,* 1866-87, pp. 15-16.
72. *Ibid.*
73. The table is based on the various District Gazetteers of Haryana.
74. K.C. Yadav: A Brief History of Development of Education in Haryana During the 19th Century, *Journal of Haryana Studies,* Vol. I, No. 2, (July-Dec. 1969), pp. 15, 17-18.
75. See *Punjab Administration Report 1882-83*; H.R. Mehta: *op. cit.*, p. 60.
76. Based on Gazetteers. See Rohtak District Gazetteer (1912), Ambala District and Kalsia State Gazetteer (1912), Gurgaon District Gazetteer (1910), Karnal District and Gazetteer (1912) and Hissar District Loharu State Gazetteer (1912).
77. Jagdish Chandra: *Freedom Movement in Haryana,* (1919-1947), p. 10.
78. *Ibid.*
79. *Punjab Native Newspapers Report,* 1919, p. 4.
80. Shri Ram Sharma: *Haryana Ka Itihas,* p. 51; Shri Ram Sharma: *Meri Apni Ram Kahani,* p. 3.

5

Political Consciousness in Haryana (1885-1918)

The Foundation of the Congress

As discussed in the earlier chapter, several factors contributed to the peoples' awakening in the later half of the 19th century. In fact, the All India National Congress, under whose banner the battle of freedom was fought was its outcome.

The establishment of the Congress in India was a definite turning point in the political history of India. Regarding its inception conflicting views have been expressed by different writers. For example, some describe it as a product of the circumstances, which had been working in India since the days of Raja Ram Mohan Roy[1], while the others call it 'a child of Russophobia.'[2] Some dub it an 'innocuous and loyal' political organisation created to serve as 'a safety-valve'[3] for the British Empire. Others regarded it as the byproduct of the prevailing popular associations in the various provinces.[4] Some attribute it to the impact of the Western education and others regard it as the creation of one man, A.O. Hume.

In fact, the idea of Indian nationalism was not a sudden affair. The origin of the Congress was the product of a combination of various factors.[5] Indian grievances were accumulating with the changing conditions of the country. The growth of English education and the impact of Western literature aroused the feeling of nationalism. It gave birth to the new English educated middle class in India. In fact it is rather an irony, a curious phenomenon, that the class which eventually became a potential factor in the India's emancipation from the British rule was the one that valued and assimilated Western literature, democratic ideas and revolutionary method. No study of freedom struggle can be completed without taking into account the role played by the English-educated class. With the initiative of this class, a number of associations[6] like the British Indian Association (Calcutta, established in 29th October, 1851), the Bombay Association (Bombay, 26th August 1852), the Bombay Presidency Association (Bombay, 29th September, 1885), the British Indian Association (North Western Provinces, Aligarh, 1867), the British Indian Association of Oudh (Lucknow, 1861), the Madras Native Association (Madras, 1852), the Madras Mahajan Sabha (Madras, January 1885), the Poona Sarvajanik Sabha (Poona, 1870), the Indian League (Calcutta, September 1875), the Western Indian Association (Bombay, 19th April 1873), and the Indian Association (Calcutta, 1876) sprang up in various provinces.

Among the various popular associations the most prominent was Indian Association which was established by the strenous efforts of S.N. Banerjee, the Moderate leader, on July 26, 1876, at Calcutta.[7] He extensively toured the country to open its branches at various places, in order to create public opinion against the reduction of the age from 21 to 19 by the Government of India for the Civil Service Examination in 1877. He also visited Lahore and Amritsar in this connection and formed a branch of the Association at Lahore.[8] The Lahore Indian Association founded in 1877 was the first political organization of importance in Punjab which included Haryana.[9] It was managed by Babu Joginder Chandra Bose, later a prominent Congress worker, and Kali Prosanna Roy, one of the first Directors of the Punjab National Bank. Undoubtedly, Indian Association played a significant role in awakening political consciousness in the country. Later in May 1884 S.N. Banerjee again visited Lahore, Amritsar, Rawalpindi, Ambala, Delhi etc.

Similarly, Lord Lytton's coercive acts increased bitterness between the Indian and the British. The virulance of plague and natural calamities and the holding of Delhi Durbar etc. increased the tendency among the educated Indian people to form some type of political organisation in order to secure their rights. Later, Lord Ripon's sympathetic and liberal attitude towards the Indians and the Ilbert Bill controversy gave the immediate impetus.[10] The *Hindu* (Madras) appealed that the political consciousness generated among the Indians during Lord Ripon's tenure should be nurtured and developed into a powerful expression of the native opinion.[11] It also called for the immediate need to affiliate the numerous associations which were scattered all over the country with a common mother association.[12]

In 1883 a Conference held under the auspices of the Indian Association at Calcutta further stimulated the desire for a political association. The leaders of political opinion looked forward to a party of all India level. In fact, it was the demand of the day, and this development could not be ignored either by Lord Dufferin or by his advisors.[13] However, it was Mr. A.O. Hume, who felt the prevailing under-currents and became convinced that some immediate and definite actions had to be taken for counteracting the growing unrest.[14] To secure the British rule in India and to inject the spirit of loyalty,[15] he tried to contain the national consciousness into constitutional channel. Consequently, the Indian National Congress was established in December, 1885.

Emergence of the Congress in Haryana

The first session of the All India Congress was held at Bombay under the roof of the Gokul Das Tejpal Sanskrit College under the chairmanship of Sir W.C. Banerjee, a leading advocate of Calcutta. In its first session it was represented by 72 delegates[16] from 27 places. Haryana was also represented by a young pleader of Ambala, Lala Murli Dhar as a representative of *The Tribune*. The other delegate from the then Punjab was the Brahmo Samaj leader, Satyanand Agnihotri. There was one more person Munshi Jwala Parshad a Pleader of Ambala[17] who took part in the first session.

Before the session, Lala Murli Dhar of Ambala made a short speech on why the Punjab needed a legislative Assembly.[18] But in the main session he remained a mere spectator and took no active part in the deliberations. But he created a sensation both by his appearance and by his speech. With his Punjabi coat and trousers and glittering cabulle turban, he presented an imposing figure. At the valedictory session he expressed the gratitude to the Bombay hosts, and brought down the hall by laying at their door the charge of theft and robbery. They had stolen and robbed his heart.[19] In 1886, at Calcutta, three delegates belonging to Haryana attended the session. They were Lala Murli Dhar of Ambala,

Pandit Din Dayalu Sharma of Jhajjar, the then editor of *The Kohnoor* (of Lahore) and Babu Balmukand Gupta of village Gudyani of Jhajjar *Tehsil* a prominent correspondent.[20] In 1887 out of the total of nine delegates from Punjab, Lala Murli Dhar represented this area. In 1888, the Congress gained some momentum when some collections of money were made in the hope that the Congress session in 1889 would be held in Punjab. *The Tribune* urged the leaders to hold the next session of the Congress in Punjab.[21] In Haryana the Congress found a new impetus with the joining of Lala Lajpat Rai, a prominent Vakil at Hissar and an Arya Samaj leader. Lala Lajpat Rai attended the session at Allahabad, in 1888, for the first time. Perhaps he was the first Indian leader, who spoke on the Congress platform in Hindi.[22] Some other notable figures of Haryana who attended the session were Chabil Dass, Gauri Shankar, and Lala Murli Dhar. In 1889 Lala Lajpat Rai also attended the Bombay session of the Congress. He met A.O. Hume, but was not impressed by him.[23] He thought that in spite of the patriotism it was hunger of the self-praise which was dominating the Congress.[24] So he remained aloof from the Congress for the next four years. But Lala Murli Dhar participated in the coming sessions.

In the session of 1891, Lala Murli Dhar exhorted the delegates to give up the foreign clothing and luxuries and to sympathise with the poor.[25] In 1892 when Lajpat Rai left Hissar and settled at Lahore for practice, the so called activites of the Congress came to its low ebb. In 1893, the first Congress in Punjab was held at Lahore. But the people did not show interest in its activites during the remaining years of the century to corne. Anyhow, it is clear from the evidences that the Congress could not gain any ground in the first decade of its inception. In the coming years also, it was not popular.

Now a pertinent question may arise, why was the Congress not popular in Haryana? Sir Michael O'Dwyer, later the Lieutenant-Governor of Punjab, once commented regarding the Punjab that though there were sporadic events of a political nature, yet on the whole it had remained politically quiescent,[26] for twenty years since the birth of the Congress in 1885, Haryana, it can be said, was politically calm in a still greater degree. In fact, the influence and impact of the Congress in Haryana was negligible.

Perhaps it was due to the fact, that educationally Haryana was one of the most backward areas of Punjab Province. As the educational facilities were not available, a vast number of the people were uneducated. There was not a single college in Haryana and only a few could get the opportunity to go either to Lahore or Delhi for higher education. Even the number of High Schools upto 1920 was only 31.[27] With the slow growth of education, there was little progress made in literature and press. So it can be said that perhaps the educational backwardness was one of the main reasons for the lesser influence of the Congress.

Similarly, Haryana being mainly rural in character, was away from the political activities of the country. Nine out of ten people were living in 6,478 villages of Haryana. There were only 30 towns with a population of more than 10,000. In fact, there was no city in Haryana in the modern sense. There were not even enough facilities of means of transport and communication. The villagers' îife for the most part, was dominated by land-owing castes such as Jats, Rajputs, Ahirs, Gujars, Meos and Ranghars. They were extensively agriculturists with little interest in political matters.

Congress only gained some ground among the few urban belts which contained the lawyers or some businessmen, mostly Hindus. But most of the population kept aloof from the Congress. Some of the Muslims of Punjab also wanted to set up a political association but Sir Syed Ahmad Khan opposed to this idea. By the turn of the century, it looked as if they held themselves aloof from all political activity. Sikhs, being a small minority, had scant choice. They were mainly busy in their social and educational activities through the Singh Sabhas.

Among the Hindus, the Arya Samaj and the Sanatan Dharma Sabha were the only notable societies in Haryana. But in the beginning, their members were more active in their social and educational programme. The Arya Samaj did not join the Congress and not participate in the political life of Haryana. The Muslim community refused to join in a national organisation, but in the beginning they did not oppose the Congress.

In short, the political activities in Haryana up to the end of the 19th century were primarily of sporadic agitation over issues affecting the social, economic and religious interests of Hindu and Muslim Communities.

Punjab Land Alienation Act

One of the most significant events in Punjab and Haryana which stimulated resentment among the dominant communities was the Punjab Land Alienation Act of 1900. The Bill proposed a lifteen years limitation on all mortgages. The limitation on mortgages was supposed to prevent money-lenders from securing possession of land without purchase and keeping it indefinitely. The second object of the Bill was the cancellation of the Zamindar's right to sell his land. The Bill established three categories of sale: permanent alienation of agricultural land to non-agriculturist be permitted only with the permission of the Collector; sale among all agricultural tribes be permitted, and the leases of land should run for a maximum period of twenty years or the life span of the lessor whichever was lesser. The Bill also suggested that the law should apply to the entire province but the local government be given the right to exempt areas and persons from its operation.[28]

From the official point of view, the object of this measure was to place restrictions on the transfer of land in the Punjab with a view to checking its alienation from the agriculture to the non-agriculture classes.[29] The legislation was to protect the *Zamindars,*[30] who had proved themselves to be the loyal section of the community, against the money-lenders. The Act was also designed to end the possibility of agitation in the rural areas,[31] and to give some relief to the peasants who were the victims of economic exploitation, famines and epidemics. The rejection of the permanent settlement of land encouraged excessive assessment, and the short-term settlement adversely affected the family life of the peasantry, especially Muslims, and encouraged rural indebtedness, and the money-lenders became a nccessary evil for them.

The Bill was strongly opposed by the press and the leaders of public opinion. it was fait that the Bill was merely a political measure which hardly aimed at the amelioration of socio economic conditions of the Muslim peasantry. It was further argued that the Bill was designed to prevent urban financial interests from acquiring the land of the hereditary peasants.[32] The Indian National Congress passed resolution against the Bill at the Lucknow session in 1899.[33] Even some of the high British official including D.C. Jhonstone, the Divisional Judge, Ambala[34], opposed the Bill.

But the Bill became law in spite of the united opposition of the Government officials, political leaders and the press. In fact, the Government pursued its own policy of "Divide and Rule" and the question assumed a communal colour.[35] Of course, it was more of a device to check the money-lenders, 'an ever-increasing political danger' than to give relief to the poor peasantry.[36] Its impact on society in general may be seen in two ways. Instead of giving relief to the poor peasants, it created a class of landed gentry which was expected to be loyal to the British Government. Secondly on the contrary, the urban Hindu middle class presented the anti-British grievances of Hindu peasants and tried to woo them away from their Muslim counterparts.[37]

The Alienation legislation angered the non-agriculturists—the money-lenders, shopkeepers and professionals, and the *Banias*—against the Government.[38] It also revived the interests of the people in the Congress which supported the urban trading class to fight against the Bill. It was called as an unwarranted intrusion on the rights of private property and a blatant attempt to make the money-lenders a scapegoat.[39] The Congress in its Lahore session in 1900 opposed the Bill.[40] It was felt that it would give new ieap to the political activity of the province. Perhaps it constituted the entry point of the Arya Samaj into politics.

On the whole, while the opposition to the Alienation Act brought the *Banias* nearer to the Congress, the rural peasants especially the Jats remained aloof from the Congress. Similarly the Brahmans stood apart from the Jats, who under the influence of the Arya Samaj were active against the orthodoxy represented by the Brahmans.[41]

Reactionary Policy of Lord Curzon

Along with the Punjab Land Alienation Act of 1900, like other provinces, Haryana witnessed a series of oppressive acts of Lord Curzon. His administrative measures came in for sharp criticism in the towns and villages of Haryana. In fact his administration was strongly attacked by the leaders of public opinion and the vernacular press. For example, Bal Mukand Gupta, a prominent Hindi writer of Haryana compared 'Curzonshahi' with 'Nadirshah' and described it as worst than that of Lord Lytton.[42] He vehementally criticised the announcement of the Partition of Bengal on July 20, 1905, which fell like a bombshell. In fact, the farewell of Lord Curzon was more welcomed than his arrival in India. In a farewell article in the *Bharta Mitra*, Balmukand Gupta summed up Lord Curzon's regime as 'a period of *Zid*.'[43]

Soon after the Partition of Bengal, the Anti-Partition agitation and the Swadeshi and Boycott movement gained impetus and soon transcended the boundaries of Bengal and assumed the character of national agitation. As early as 1891 Lala Murli Dhar had given a call to give up foreign clothing.[44] He again voiced his views in the 1894 Congress Session.[45] A vigorous campaign was launched against the foreign cloth, the use of foreign sugar etc. People were urged to take up the cause of Swadeshi in the principal towns of Haryana. *The Tribune* appealed to the people to solemnly pledge themselves not to touch English articles.[46] A series of meetings were held in different towns in Haryana. For example at Rohtak a meeting of Jain youngmen was held on the day of *Dussehra* festival in which Lala Jauhre Mal, a pleader, presided and where a draper pledged to denounce selling German or Italian cloth. In October 17, 1905 a meeting was held at Lahore to form the Punjab Swadeshi Association.[47] Its object was said to encourage and improve the manufacture and provide information about the indigenous articles in the following manner:[48]

(*a*) By taking pledges.

(*b*) By opening Indian stores and show rooms.

(*c*) By the collection of information, arranging for lectures, publishing papers, distributing literature and adopting such other means as may be found necessary.

(*d*) By introducing machines, particularly those worked by hands.

It was decided that a company be established with limited liability to manufacture, sell and let handlooms do all other things. It was calculated to promote the weaving industry in the province, and float stores for the sale of the Swadeshi goods.[49] It was further resolved that a mass meeting be held on 22nd October, and a procession be taken out on the same day.[50]

Consequently, on 21st October a largely attended meeting of the Swadeshi Company took place in Hindu Hall at Ambala City under the presidentship of Lala Murli Dhar in which Lala Beni Prasad and Lala Dwarka Dass also participated.[51] Similar meetings were held at Ambala Cantt., and other places.

In fact, the Swadeshi Movement sprang rapidly from one end of the country to the other within an incredibly short time. Lajpat Rai rightly wrote:

> "When 100 years lip agitation and paper agitation failed, in these six months or twelve months right work has succeeded."[52]

Lajpat Rai's Arrest and Deportation

With the termination of Lord Curzon's tenure and coming of Lord Minto, the new Viceroy of India, the unrest did not subside. Rather it increased due to the economic hardships, the impact of natural calamities like famine and plague and a number of repressive measures. Some legislations like the Punjab Limitation Act, 1904, the Transfer of Property Act, 1904 and the Punjab Pre-emption Act, 1905, were passed to weaken the position of the money-lenders. The Punjab Land Alienation Act Amendaient Bill, 1906 was a further attempt to strengthen alienation restrictions. It generated political discontent, especially among the Hindu commercial castes. It was considered by them as an 'act of great injustice and hardship' and a 'breach of faith'.[54] It spread political unrest and generated bitterness.

Like the Punjab Land Alienation Act Amendment Bill, the Colonization of Government Lands Punjab Bill 1906, further weakened the communal ties. It provided the leaders of public opinion with an occasion to mobilize support for anti-government activities. In fact, the Bill mainly concerned the newly set-up area of Chenab and Jhelum colonies of the Punjab.[55] It was proposed to check a further division of the land, which was resented by the people as an unjustified interference in their time bound customs and traditions.[56] The Bill became law on 5th March 1907 despite strong opposition and intense popular agitation in Punjab. Similarly the enhancement of the land revenue assessment in Rawalpindi District and also the occupier's rate on the Doab Canal led to the increase of tension.[57]

The tension among people had been accentuated due to the unparalleled virulance of plague, 'which caused the death rate in 1907 to rise to 62.1 per thousand'. This death rate was the highest recorded since the establishment of the system of registration forty-one years ago.[58] In a telegram, Lord Minto, the Viceroy, informed the Secretary of State for India:

"... The horrible ravages of the plague are raising all sorts of wild suspicion against us; that we are poisoning the wells and are determined to kill off a percentage of the people."[59]

In a private letter to his wife, Minto mentioned that in the Punjab alone there were over 54,000 deaths in a week.[60] Soon it spread throughout the country and took about two million lives by 1910.[61]

These economic hardships and privation perpetuated by nature producing widespread resentment against the authorities. Like Punjab, in Haryana region also many largely attended public meetings were held at various places. Though the main nucleus of the activities remained Punjab, but it effected the people of Haryana also.

On 16th April 1907, a riot broke out at Lahore, when the Chief Court of Punjab sentenced K.K. Athavale to simple imprisonment in the *Panjabee* case. Pindi Das, the editor of the weekly *India* appearing from Gujranwala was also sentenced to imprisonment for publishing a letter from America inciting seditions among the Indian troops.

The police party escorting Athavale and Pindi Das from the Court to the jail was attacked by a crowd of resentful students which stopped the carriage and garlanded the convicts. In an article, Balmukand Gupta, a prominent writer of Haryana, admired the courage and heroic imprisonment of Athavale and Pindi Das.[62]

Sir Denzil Ibbetson, the Lieutenant-Governor of Panjab, regarded the political situation in Punjab as 'exceedingly serious, and 'cxceedingly dangerous', which urgently demanded a remedy. He sensed that *Nai-Hawa* (New climate) was blowing through men's minds in all the districts of Punjab.

Consequently, Lajpat Rai and Sardar Ajit Singh were arrested at Lahore on account of their 'seditious' speeches and articles and deported without trial in the middle of 1907.

Lajpat's deportation generated a new spirit and stirred up men's mind in Haryana. This high handed act of the Government in arresting one of the most respected leaders shook the faith of the people in constitutional methods. The press made a virulent attack on this action. *The Tribune* commented on the episode as follows:

"The country does not approve of the adoption of methods which are, today the least un-English and unworthy of a civilised Government such as others.[63]

The *Jan Ratan* (Ambala)[64] commented;
"Bharat Mata weeps and cries
I have lost my honour and respect
The Swan has been carried away from the Garden of India.
To whom the nightangle of union was so deeply devoted."

At this juncture, Bal Mukand Gupta made an cryptic appeal in the following Hindi poem:[65]

सबके सब पंजाबी अब हैं लायलटी में चकनाचूर,
सारा ही पंजाब देश बन जाने को है लायलपुर।
लायल हैं सब सिक्ख अरोड़े खतरी भी लायल हैं,
मेड, रहातिया, बनिये धुनिंया लायल ही के कायल हैं

लायल सब वकील बरिस्टर जमीदार और लाला हैं,
म्युनिसिपलटियां वाले तो लायलटी का परनाला हैं।
खान बहादुर राय बहादुर कितने ही सरदार नवाब,
सब मिलकर जुलकर लूट रहे हैं लायलटी का खूब शबाब।

ऐरा गैरा नत्थू खैरा सब पर इसकी मस्ती है,
लायलटी लाहौर अब भूसे से भी कुछ सस्ती है।
केवल दो डिस-लायल थे वे एक लाजपत एक अजीत,
दोनों गये निकाले उनसे नहीं किसी की है कुछ प्रीत।

The impact[66] of the arrest of Lala Lajpat Rai was not only local but it aroused feelings of resentment throughout the country. Public meetings protesting against their arrest were held at various places. Anyhow, Lajpat Rai's arrest increased his prestige and reputation. Now his name became popular and known in the ranks of the national leaders. His arrest aroused political consciousness and hatred towards British and shook the faith of the people in the British set up.

Reyolutionary Activities and Repression

The deportation of Lajpat Rai without any substantial charges having been levelled against him, stirred up the revolutionary movement in Haryana also. The practice of deportation had always 'stuck in the throat of the Secretary of State' because 'it outraged his liberal conscience'. On the suggestion of Morley, Minto released both Lajpat Rai and Ajit Singh on I8th November 1907.

But their release did not subside the anti-government propaganda. Sardar Ajit Singh vigorously campaigned for the establishment of a network of revolutionary societies. He tried to form secret societies almost in all the principal towns of the Punjab.[67] He had planned to start a paper called *'The Lion of the Punjab'*.[68] He also published two books entitled *Mohibhan-i-Watan* (Patriots of the country) and *Mutalba Mal* (Demand of Land tax) in January 1908.[69] But Sardar Ajit Singh had to flee to Persia when the Government tried to arrest him again.

Pandit Nekhi Ram Sharma a prominent leader of Haryana wrote an article entitled *Vipati Par Vipati* (calamity after calamity) which was published in the *Abhivudaya* (Allahabad). In it he criticised the land revenue policy of the government. Consequently, the government was alarmed and Mr. Joseph, the Deputy Commissioner, Rohtak, warned him for his anti-British activities.[70]

The year 1909 witnessed the explosion of a bomb at the house of Mr. Sykes, the Deputy Collector, Ambala. Perhaps this was the first serious revolutionary action in Haryana. On the night of December 29, 1909, a servant of Mr. Sykes found a tin case on a road leading to his master's house,[71] which he took to his house and opened it in the compound. The tincase contained a bomb which exploded badly shattering the man's hand.[72]

However, the Punjab Government became alarmed from the very beginning. The repressive methods adopted by the authorities included the prosecution of the press, and ban on papers, pamphlets, books, circulars etc., the arrests and deportations, prohibition of public meetings and the encouragement to the loyalists.[73]

The Government of India passed the Seditious Meetings Act which banned not only the political activities, but also restrained the religious activities. Though it had not been applicable to Punjab, Rohtak district was declared to be a proclaimed area under the prevention of seditions Meetings Act.[74] But the repressive measures did not succeed in crushing the sentiments of the people.

The Minto Morley Reforms

Lord Minto submitted a draft to Morley and made certain proposals to reconcile educated Indian opinion. In 1908 the 'Minto-Morley Reforms' were announced. The opening of the door to communal representation[75] was neither liked by the moderâtes nor by the extremists, but was welcomed by the Muslim League. At a session of the Ail India Congress at Lahore held in 1909, Pandit Madan Mohan Malaviya devoted his speech mainly to the repercussions and results of the Reform Act.[76] It was logical that the doctrine of communal representation was bound to create tension and conflicts in various communities.

The people cf Haryana were also disappointed with the provision of the Reforms. The feeling of the people may be summed up in the following words of a prominent writer of Haryana.

> "Not only today, but since the last year Mr. Morlev had been giving assurances for the 'reforms'. But with what results?"

In accordance to Minto Morley Reforms, two members were taken from Haryana in the Punjab Legislative Assembly. They were Rai Bahadur Jawahar Lal Bhargava, Advocate from Hissar and Rao Bahadur Chaudhry Lal Chand, Advoctate of Rohtak.

The First World War

With the outbreak of the 1st World War, India, being a part of the British Empire was also dragged in it. The people of Haryana helped the Government by providing recruits and by contributing money and material. Haryana's contribution to the army personnel was 71,366[78] which was nearly 1/5 of the total number raised in Punjab.[79] The following table shows progress recruitment. (See Table at Page 93).

In the sphere of recruitment, all kinds of inducements were held out to those who brought in the recruits. Public rewards were given to those who helped the Government. Almost in every district *Durbars* were held. It was in a *Durbar* held by Sir Michael O'Dwyer in Haryana that the Government assured That it would dig Bhakhara Dam Canal which would change the face of Haryana.[80] Major rewards for war services,[81] were given as shown on Page 94.

Statement Showing Progress of Recruiting by Division, Districts for each Stage of Campaign according to returns of Divisions Recruiting Offices

Division or District	*Combatants in the Indian Army on 1st Jan. 1915*	*4th August 1915 — 3 1st March 1916.*	*1st Jan. 1917 — 30th June 1917*	*1st July, 1917 — 31st Dec. 1917.*	*1st Jan. 1918 — 3 1st May 1918*	*1st June 1918 — 30th Nov. 1918*	*Total Nos. of Indian Army and Imperial Service troops on 30th Nov. 1918*
Hissar	3,046	2,795	1,438	4,589	1,251	3,698	15,461
Rohtak	6,245	5,025	3,014	3,661	1,546	3,950	22,144
Gurgaon	2,481	3,440	2,241	4,048	2,184	4,869	18,867
Karnal	633	532	635	1,413	683	3,005	6,553
Ambala	1,755	1,256	482	989	1,893	2,070	8,341
Haryana Region	14,160	13,048	7,810	14,750	7,557	17,592	71,366
Total British Districts of Punjab	80,146	64,519	27,301	56,342	55,143	76,532	361,886

See M.S. leigh: *The Punjab and the War 1922*, p. 59.

District	Number of Persons	Villages	Titles	Sword of Honour	Seats in Durbar	Jagir worth Rs.	Square or rectangle of land	Recruiting Badge
Hissar	35	33	12	2	3	1500	52	7
Rohtak	46	46	15	6	2	1500	79	13
Gurgaon	28	28	5	6	2	950	44	19
Karnal	30	28	6	2	2	—	76	6
Ambala	49	48	13	3	4	—	145	6
Haryana Region	178	183	51	19	13	3,950	396	51
British Districts of Punjab and Haryana.	1,035	903	310	86	56	20,450	2,750	286

The above list does not include the long lists of awards to the officials belonging to various departments.

A Recruiting Centre was opened at Delhi specially for the jats of Haryana. Jhajjar, Rewari and Bhiwani were centres of recruits. In fact, in this way, the communal feeling was encouraged. Later on, it was replaced by the territorial system of recruitment through which men of any class could be enrolled in every district.

Coercive methods were also used with a view to enlisting recruits.[82] The System of purchase of recruits was adopted. Proposals for conscription methods were also made.[83] But the Government of India rejected the idea of conscription on political grounds.[84]

To provide more recruitment, attempts were made to encourage loyalty. Indian officials and respectables were employed in recruiting work in each district. Honours and Commissions were given to them by the Government. Some of the notable who helped the Government very much were Sir Chhotu Ram, Chaudhry Lal Chand and Pandit Prabhu Dayal, of Rohtak, Rao Balbir Singh of Gurgaon, Chaudhry Lajpat Rai of Hissar and Choudhry Bansgopal of Karnal.[85]

As regards the war funds and war loans[86] Haryana made a notable contribution. The total war loan as collected district-wise was as follows:

District	*War-loan in Rupees*
Ambala	25,96,441
Karnal	24,45,226
Gurgaon	15,99,118
Rohtak	24,12,865
Hissar	82,90,016
Native States	12,90,000
	Total 1,86,33,666

The war-loan had been described by O'Dwyer as 'Phal-nale-phallian'[87] (honour with profit). A day was fixed in Haryana in order to collect the funds. In Haryana it was popularly known as *Aur De* (give more) and the people of Haryana contributed generously to it. The highest individual contribution made in the province was 10 lakhs from Rai Bahadur Sukh Lal of Bhiwani; and 4.5 lakhs from Rai Sahib Tara Chand, both of the Hissar district; whereas the wife of the former subscribed another one lakh to the women's section of the loan.[88] The town of Bhiwani, which had initially promised ₹ 15 lakhs as loans, contributed ₹ 25 lakhs.[89] It was the highest contributions made in proportion to the population.

Though the people of Haryana helped the British Government in war efforts, yet the Government paid no attention towards their hardships. Just after the war services of nearly 15,500 soldiers from Haryana were terminated in the wake of demobilisation. They were deprived of their earning and were not provided any re-employment.

The war upset the economic situation of the region. It was officially[90] admitted that rising of prices and increase of taxation were causes of dis-affection among the masses. The inflation without a proportionate increase in production had resulted in high prices and devaluation of money.[91] Price of wheat and flour increased.[92] Cheap grain shops could not check the rising prices.[93] During 1912-1919, the prices of wheat, barley, jowar, bajra, (gram) and maize, which were largely consumed by the poorer classes, rose enormously as is indicated below:[94]

Commodity	*Retail prices during the fort-night ending 15th Dec. 1912 (for a rupee) Seerschittaks*	*Retail prices during the fort-night ending 15th Jan. 1919 (for a rupee) Seerschittaks*
Wheat	12-4	6-9
Barley	15-13	8-3
Jowar	15-12	4-3
Bajra	12-3	4-2
Gram	15-1	7-7
Maize	16-1	6-6

As compared with 1894 the price of food-stuffs had risen five times by 1919.[95] Besides, other commodities became rare. Government made efforts to help the people by prohibiting the export of grain, by selling salt at cheaper rates, by retailing of cheaper cloth and control of the sale of kerosene.[96] But these measures could provide nominal relief to the people living in towns only. In fact, the villages were totally neglected.[97]

Then the natural calamities like floods, plague and influenza increased their tension. It has been calculated that in a few months influenza carried off half a million of Punjab's population, whereas about 30,000 from Punjab lost their lives in the war. It caused more havoc in a few months than bubonic plague during the previous twenty years.[98] The districts of Gurgaon and Rohtak suffered heavily in the whole of Punjab and the death rates were the highest.[99]

During the war, the people of Haryana could not actively participate in any national movement. It was due to the reason that the rural masses took more interest in war than in the movement. The people of Haryana could not hear the inspiring song of the Ghadar Party. However Lala Kashi Ram[100] of Ambala District was one of the architects of the Ghadar Party in Sanfrancico with Hardyal. He returned to India in 1914. He was arrested by the British and on 27th Nov., 1915 was hanged. Perhaps he was the first Haryanvi martyr in this phase of the freedom movement. His property worth ₹ 40,000 was confiscated by the government. Likewise, some leaders like Pandit Neki Ram Sharma showed keen interest in Home Rule Agitation. Some activities were held at Rohtak and Bhiwani. But with the arrest of Pandit Neki Ram Sharma[101] in July 1918, when he defied the prohibitary order at

Delhi by holding a public meeting at Birla Mandir Dharmshala, the Home Rule Agitation also subsided in Haryana.

In the meanwhile, it can be said that during 1917-18 the Congress began to gain roots in Haryana. In 1917 the Congress committee was establislied at Rohtak. Chaudhry Chhotu Ram and Babu Shyam Lal were its first President and Sccretary respectively. In 1917 at the Calcutta session of the Congress, five people of Rohtak represented the district. Besides, Pandit Neki Ram Sharma not only participated, but impressed the audience in the session by his emotional speech.

In 1918, when the people of Haryana were disgusted with the economic hardships, particularly the *Begar*, it was Pandit Neki Ram Sharma who took initiative against this social and economic evil. He was the first political leader in Haryana who opposed this exploitation of the poor. He visited various places in Haryana. Perhaps, in a sense, this was the first movement which created political consciousness among the people of Haryana.

The people of Haryana took part with great vigour in the Congress session which was held at Delhi in 1918 under the Presidentship of Pandit Madan Mohan Malaviya. Pandit Neki Ram Sharma and Chaudhry Peru Singh, Lala Shyam Lal, Sardar Buta Singh and Lala Daulat Ram participated in this session. Establishment of the Congress Committees at various places generated a new spirit and consciousness among the masses.

To sum up, it can be said that though the people of Haryana rnade substantial contribution in the war, yet they experienced infinite sufferings and privations in return. The coercive methods used in recruitment and war-loans prepared the ground for the great upheaval. The problem of unemployment further complicated the issue. Natural calamities like plague and influenza coupled with the economic hardships shook the confidence of the pensants. Now the political atmosphere was surcharged with tension and it only require the political conscious leaders to exploit the opportunity of mobilising the public opinion against the policies of the government.

NOTES

1. S.R. Singh: Russophobia and lhe Foundation of Congress, *The Indian History Congress, Proceedings*, (24th Session, 1961), p. 241, *see also* Pattabhi Sitaramayya: *History of the Indian National Congress*, Vol. I, (Delhi, 1965), p. 19.

2. Dr. Nand Lal Chatterji: The Foundation of the Congress and Russophobia, *Journal of Indian History*, Vol. XXXVI, Pt. II, pp. 171-77.
3. Lajpat Rai: *Young India*, p. 137.
4. For a detailed study of popular associations see S.R. Mehrotra: *The Emergence of the Indian National Congress*, (Delhi, 1971), pp. 148- 229.
5. G.N. Singh: *Landmarks in Indian Constitutional and National Movement* (1600-1919), p.; P.N. Chopra: Genesis and Growth of Indian National Congress, *Journal of Indian History*, Vol. I, Pt. II, (August, 1972), p. 389.
6. For detail see S.R. Mehrotra; *op. cit*., p. 148.
7. C.F. Andrews and Girija Mukherjee: *The Rise and Growth of Congress in India*, p. 64; S R. Mehrotra: *op. cit*., p. 164; S.N. Banerjee: *A Nation in Making*, p. 38.
8. Daniel Argov: *Moderates and Extremists in the India National Movement*, p. 4; J.C. Bagal: *History of Indian Association*, (Calcutta 1952), pp. 22-31.
9. S.N. Banerjee: *A Nation in Making*, (Reprint, Calcutta, 1963), p. 13.
10. S.R. Singh, *op, cit*., p. 240.
11. *The Hindu*, 26-12-1884.
12. Ranga Swami Parthasarthy; *A Hundred Years of the Hindu, The Epie Story of Indian Nationalism*, (Madras, 1978), p. 30.
13. Briton, Martin: *New India, 1885*, (Barkeley, 1969), p. 42.
14. A.C. Majumdar: *Indian National Evolution*, p. 46.
15. B.L. Grover: *A Documentary Study of British Policy towards Indian Nationalism (1885-1909)*, (Delhi, 1969), p. 17.
16. Some writers have given the number of actual representation as 71, which is not correct.
17. *Report of the First National Congress, 1885*, (Available at All India Congress Committee Library, New Delhi).
18. *The Tribune*, 19-12-1885.
19. See *Reis and Rayyet*, (A Calcutta Weekly), Quoted by S.R. Mehrotra: *op-cit*., p. 417.
20. S.R. Sharma: *Haryana Ke Itihas*, p. 48.
21. *The Tribune*, 4-7-1888.
22. S.C. Mittal: *Deshratan Lala Lajpat Rai*, p. 14.
23. *Ibid*.
24. *Ibid*.
25. *Report of the Indian National Congress for 1891*, p. 21.
26. Sir Michael O'Dwyer: *India as I knew it*, p. 27; B.C. Pal: *Beginning of Freedom Movement in Modern India*, p. 25; Azim Husain: *Fazi-i-Husain, A Political Biography*, pp. 70 and 77.
27. Jagdish Chander: *Freedom Struggle in Haryana (1919-1947)*, p. 10.
28. S.R. Sharma: *Punjab in Ferment*, p. 26.
29. *Ibid*.
30. Norman Gerald Barrier: *Punjab Politics and the Disturbances of 1907*, p. 82.
31. *Ibid*.
32. Mark Naidis: *The Punjab Disturbances in 1919*, p. 21.

33. Jagdish S. Sharma: *India's Struggle for Freedom*, Vol. I, p. 8.
34. *Legislative Department Proceedings*, Nos. 11-62, (October 1900), p. 1.
35. Satya M. Rai: *Partition of the Punjab*, p. 24; Tara Chand: *History of Freedom Movement in India*, Vol. II, p. 299.
36. Lord Curzon: *Speeches*, Vol. II, pp. 124-5.
37. H.F. Owen: Towards Nationwide Agitation and Organisation, The Home Rule League 1915-18, *Sounding in Modern South Asian History*, (Ed. by D.A. Low), pp. 161-62.
38. H. Calvart: *Wealth and Welfare of the Punjab*, (Lahore, 1922), p. 137.
39. N.G. Barrier: *Punjab Politics and the Disturbances of 1907*, p. 87.
40. K.L. Gauba: *Harkishan Lal*, p. 25.
41. Jagdish Chander: *op. cit.*, p. 23.
42. Ranjit Singh: Babu Lal Bal Mukand Gupta Ka Swadesh Prem: Ek Adhyan, *Journal of Haryana Studies*, Vol. II, Nos. 1-2, 1970, p. 122.
43. *Ibid.*, p. 123.
44. *Report of the Indian National Congress for 1891*, p. 21.
45. *Report of the Indian National Congress for 1894*, p. 58.
46. *The Tribune*, 2-9-1905
47. *The Panjabee*, 16-10-1905.
48. *Ibid.*
49. For detail *see* S.C. Mittal: *Freedom Movement in Punjab*, pp. 23-28; *The Panjabee*. 16-10-1905.
50. *The Panjabee*, 16-10-1935.
51. *Ibid.*, 30-10-1905.
52. V.C. Joshi (Ed.): *Lajpat Rai, Writings and Speeches*, Vol. I. 128.
53. Satya Rai: *Partition of the Punjab*, p. 28.
54. S.R. Sharma: *Punjab in Ferment*, p. 68.
55. For detail *see* S.C. Mittal: *Freedom Movement in Punjab*, pp. 41-45.
56. Siyed Razi Wasti: *Lord Minto and the Indian Nationl Movement*, p. 94.
57. *Punjab Administration Report*, 1907-8, p. iv.
58. *Ibid.*, p. viii.
59. Mary Minto (Countess of): *India Minto and Morley*, (London, 1909) p. 126.
60. *Ibid.*, p. 135.
61. Edward Thompson and G.T. Garratt; *Rise and Fulfilment of British Rule in India*, (1966), p. 561.
62. Ranjit Singh: Babu Bal Mukand Gupta Ka Swadesh Prem: Ek Adhyan, *Journal of Haryana Studies*, Vol. II, Nos. 1-2, 1970, pp. 119-20.
63. *The Tribune*, 29-5-1907.
64. S.C. Mittal: Lala Lajpat Rai's Deportation and the Growth of Public Opinion, *Kurukshetra University Research Journal*, Vol. VIII, Nos. 1-2, 1974. pp. 72-73.
65. Ranjit Singh: Balmukand Gupta Ka Swadesh Prem: Ek Adhyan, *Journal of Haryana Studies*, Vol. II, Nos. 1-2, 1970, p. 127.
66. S.C. Mittal: Lala Lajpat Rai's Deportation and the Growth of Public Opinion, *Kurukshetra University Research Journal*, Vol. VIII, Nos. 1-2 1974, p. 74.

67. Home Department (*Political-B*), *Govt. of India, Proceedings,* July 1908, Nos. 72-81.
68. Home Department (*Political-B*) *Govt. of India Proceedings,* January 1908, Nos. 111-118.
69. Home Department (*Political-B*) *Govt. of India, Proceedings,* February 1908, Nos. 105-112.
70. M.M. Juneja: *op. cit.,* pp. 6-7; *The Abhinanden Grantlt,* p. 20.
71. Home Department (*Political-B*), *Govt. of India Proceedings,* March 1910, Nos. 109-117.
72. *Ibid.,* Mary Minto (Countess of), *op. cit.,* p. 367.
73. S.C. Mittal: *Freedom Movement in Punjab,* p. 64.
74. Home Department (*Political-Deposit*), *Govt. of India, Proceedings,* March 1911, No. 1.
75. A.B. Keith: *The Constitutional History of India,* pp. 228-32; G.N. Singh: *op. cit.,* pp. 200-213.
76. Jagdish S. Sharma: *op. cit.,* Vol. I. pp. 369-70.
77. Ranjit Singh: Bal Mukand Gupta Ka Swadesh Prem: Ek Adhyan, *Journal of Haryana Studies,* Vol. II, Nos. 1-2, 1970, p. 127.
78. M.S. Leigh: *The Punjab and the War,* p. 59.
79. Total Punjab's contribution to the Army personnel was 361,886 which was more than half of the total number raised in India. Jagdish Chander is incorrect that Haryana provided a little less than half of the total recruits in Punjab. *See* Jagdish Chander: *op. cit.,* p. 24.
80. Shri Ram Sharma: *Haryana Ka Itihas,* p. 56.
81. M.S. Leigh: *op, cit.,* pp. 140-74.
82. Home Department (*Polilical-B*), *Govt. of India Proceedings,* June 1918, Nos. 401-4.
83. Home : Department (*Political-Deposit*), *Govt. of India; Proceedings,* August 1918, No. 28.
84. V.N. Datta; *Jallianwala Bagh,* p. 13.
85. Shri Ram Sharma: *Haryana Ka Itihas,* p. 55.
86. Jagdish Chander: *op. cit.,* p. 25.
87. *Punjab Legislative Council Proceedings* April, 1917, p. 223.
88. Home Department (*Political Deposit*), *Govt. of India, Proceedings,* October 1918, No. 32.
89. *Ibid.*
90. *The Disorder Inquiry Committee, Minute of Evidence,* Vol. III, *See Written Statements,* pp. 1-179.
91. *Punjab Legislative Council, Proceedings,* 6th March 1920, p. 76.
92. Home Department (*Political Deposit*), *Govt. of India, Proceedings,* January 1915, No. 43.
93. Home Department (*Political Deposit*), *Govt. of India Proceedings,* September 1915, No. 5.
94. Peary Mohan: *An Imaginery Rebellion, How it was Suppressed,* p. 36; *See* S.C. Mittal, *Freedom Movement in Punjab,* p. 101.

95. Peary Mohan; *op. cit.*, p. 36.
96. *Ibid.*
97. *The Tribune*, 25-1-1919.
98. Edward Thompson and G.A. Garratt: *op. cit.*, p. 544.
99. Donald W. Ferrell: The Rowlatt Satyagraha in Delhi, *Essays on Gandhian Politics : The Rowlatt Satyagraha of 1919*, (Ed. by Ravindra Kumar), p. 198.
100. For detail *see* S.C. Mittal: Pandit Kashi Ram, Ghadar Party Ke Mahan Neta, *Jan Sahitya*, June 1972, pp. 62-63.
101. M.M. Juneja: *op, cit.*, p. 11.

6

Intensive Movements in Haryana (1919—1929)

The year 1919 witnessed a wave of unrest and distrust. The people had ungrudgingly brooked all types of miseries during the war and made common cause with the British in a war which was fought in the name of democracy. These factors, coupled with the tall promises made by the British, had roused high expectations. But while the people expected a reward for their services, the newly acquired victory over an enemy so formidable had roused the British ego to a new height and stiffened their neck beyond all proportions. The people expected right to self-determination and due consideration of India's claim for self-government[1], and they got the Rowlatt Bills and the Montagu-Chelmsford Report. Mrs. Annie Besant on the very day of the publication of the later, condemned it as it was 'unworthy of England to offer and unworthy of India to accept'. At the Indian National Congress Session, the report was criticised as 'inadequate, disappointing and unsatisfactory'. While the coercive methods adopted by the Government, the natural calamities and economic hardships frustrated the peasants, the imposition of Income and Excess Profits Taxes and the Co-operative Society Acts also upset the trading and business classes.[2] People of small fixed income and the Government servants were discontended due to the rising prices.[3] Similarly, the educated classes were distrusted due to O'Dwyer's stringent actions and his inflammatory and irritating speeches. Sir Michael O'Dwyer, the Lieutenant-Governor of Punjab, had denounced concept of self-government in the following words: "India would not be fit for self-government much before doomsday."[4] The Muslims were irritated at the humiliating treatment accorded to Turkey by the Allies. In fact the surcharged political atmosphere of the country required asympathetic and tactful handling.

Rowlatt Bills Agitation

With the publication of the Montford Report, on the same day the Sedition Committee Report was also published. The Rowlatt committee was appointed on 10th February 1917 by Lord Chelmsford, the Viceroy of India, to investigate into the revolutionary movement in India and to make recommendations accordingly to crush it. It held 46 sittings and submitted its 226 pages report on 15th April 1918. It surveyed the revolutionary activities in India and recommended that certain drastic powers be given to the executive authority of the Government of India. Consequently, the Government of India drafted two Bills and presented them to the Imperial Legislative Council on 18th January 1919. This move was universally opposed by Indians of all shades of political opinion. It was severely criticised even by all the non-official Indian Members-elected or nominated.[5] For example, Mr. V. J. Patel called these Bills as one of the 'blunders'[6] and 'grave menace to public liberty.'[7] M.A. Jinnah giving various arguments against the Bills described them as 'unprecedented or unparalleled in any other civilized country.'[8] Dr. Tej Bahadur Sapru described them as 'wrong in principle, unsound in its conception and dangerous in its operation.'[9] Pt. Madan Mohan Malaviya compared these unpopular Bills with the Prevention of Crimes Act 1882 which was passed for the Ireland and called it 'more drastic.'[10] Similarly the other Muslim leaders also attacked the Bills; Khan Bahadur Mian Muhammed Shafi described the Bills as 'unjustinable, unnecessary and inopportune.'[11] Raja of Mahmmodabad described these Bills as 'unopportune, unsound, uncalled for and un-British,'[12] and called them as 'a question of life and death,'[13] to himself. Mr. Mazhar-ul-Haque declared them as a 'negation of all law', 'dangerously inexpedient' and 'entirely inopportune' and according to him it had 'no urgency to be passed'. Even the moderate leader Sir S. N. Banerjee requested the Government of India 'to drop them altogether.[15]

These Bills came as 'a rude shock' to Gandhiji.[16] 'Its recommendation startled me,'[17] said Gandhi. He described these bills as 'unmistakable symptom of deep-seated disease in the governing body.' He called for an All India agitation in support of the demand for the withdrawal of the Bills.

These 'Black Bills' generated a 'wave of anger,'[18] throughout the country. The Indian Press condemned the Bills in the severest terms. *The Tribune* described their introduction as a 'blunder of colossal magnitude[19].'

Gandhi decided that a general *hartal* be observed throughout the country. March 30 was first fixed as the date of the *hartal* but it was soon changed to April 6.

In Haryana, the Bills-were called *Kale Qanun* (Black laws). Protest meetings were held. Resolutions were passed urging the Government to withdraw the Bills. In a meeting held at Ambala on 11th February 1919, it was said that the Bills if passed into laws, will be wholly subversive of the elementary and fundamental rights of the British citizenship.[20] Similar resolutions were also passed at Hissar, Hansi, Rohtak, Bhiwani, Palwal and several other towns of Haryana.[21]

The Satyagraha Samitis were constituted in every town. The people resolved that if the Bills became law, they would civily refuse to obey these laws, and refrain from violence to life and property. Under these committees a series of public meetings were held. In some of the meetings the people wore black badges.

Now it emerged as a nation-wide movement. All the prominent leaders of Haryana also participated in the movement. In Haryana the Satyagraha movement was led by the local leaders. For example, at Rohtak, it was led by Chaudhry Peru Singh and Chhotu Ram. One of the main source of inspiration in Haryana was the active participation of Swami Sharddhanand of Delhi. Under his leadership, the Arya Samajists whole heartedly threw themselves in the movement. In fact, his entry into the movement was a great success of Gandhiji.

On March 30, complete *hartals* were observed at Hissar, Gurgaon, Rohtak, Panipat, Karnal and Ambala.[23] According to Major Ferrar, Delhi was responsibe for nine-tenth of the unrest in Punjab.[24] Similarly Mr. H. K. Trevaskis, the Deputy Commissioner, Gurgaon, admitted that the Delhi propaganda effected the Municipal areas. Pressure was exercised by the Delhi *Banias* on local *banias* to start *hartal* by refusing *hundis*, threatening to break off marriage and other connections.[25] Local *Banias* also put pressure on the *Zamindars* to join the demonstration in favour of *hartal*.[26] A number of emissaries were also sent from Delhi to stir up the people.[27]

In Rohtak, the Arya Samaj played a dynamic role among the Jats, who were the dominant community in the district.[28] The English educated youngmen were the main organisers of the Satyagraha-Hartal movement.[29] Newspapers like the '*Vijaya*' and '*Congress*' created an atmosphere of agitation. The leaders of the movement like Maulvi Bashir-Ahmed of Delhi and Pandit Tola Ram cf Aligarh toured the Rohtak District. The trading classes adopted the practice of dishonouring the *hundis* of those persons who stood out against the movement.[30] In fact, 'the movement was so strong and so far reaching that no single private person in the Rohtak district was able to stand out against it.[31]

On 2nd and 3rd April, at Ambala, it was decided to hold a *hartal* in the city on the 6th April. Leaders of agitation were Lala Tara Chand, Lala Nand Kishore and Muhammed Hanif.[32]

Consequently on 6th April 1919, the *hartals* were observed througbout the region particularly in Hissar and Bhiwani. At Hissar the *hartal* was organised by Shyam Lal and Bakshi Ram Krishan with the help of Hindu Club. At Bhiwani it was led by Pandit Neki Ram Sharma, K. A. Desai and Ram Kumar Bidhat, with the help of Yuvak Mandal.[33] In a public meeting at Bhiwani the people pledged to help the agitation unless and until it was repeaied.[34] *Hartals* were also observed at Rohtak, and Sonepat. The anger of the people against the British can be gleened from the fact that the carpenters of Rohtak refused to make a biar of Reverend Carlyon, a Christian missionary and no labour came forward to dig his grave.[35] His last journey was therefore delayed by about six hours.[36] *Hartals* were also observed during 6th to 10th April at all important towns like Ballabhgarh, Gurgaon, Faridabad, Palwal, Rohtak, Jhajjar, Sonepat, Rewari, Panipat, Thanesar, Ambala, Jagadhari, Ladwa and Karoal.[37] On 11th in a mass meeting at Gaukarna Tank at Rohtak sale of proscribed literature was advocated and a Joint Hindu-Mohammedan Committee was formed. On 12th at Beri the *hartal* was observed.

In the meanwhile a number of events excited a wave of anger and intensified the whole movement. The first in the series was the firing at the Railway Station, Delhi by the police on 30th March, which resulted in the death of a few persons and a large number of the people received injuries. Later, Swami Sharddhanand not only led a huge procession, but also faced the police and shouted. 'Main Khara hun goli Maro' (I am here, shoot.)'[38] This act of bravery on the part of Sharddhanand gave new impetus to the movement. Sharddhanand emerged as one of the most popular national leaders.[39] Even the Government of India could not remove him from Delhi.[40]

The second event was the arrest of Gandhi at Palwal on 9th April 1919. He was served with a notice by O'Dwyer, the Lieutenant-Governor of Punjab prohibiting his entry into Haryana. Gandhi protested, but he was arrested and sent back to Bombay under the police escort. His arrest aroused wave of unrest and excitement.[41]

On 13th April 1919 the cold-blooded massacre took place at Jallianwala Bagh, Amritsar. In fact that event not only intensified but changed the nature and character of the movement. Like the towns of Punjab, a number of violent incidents took place at Ambala, Karnal and Rohtak. Telegraph wires were cut on the North-Western Railway near Barara station (in Ambala District) on 14th April.[42] At Bahadurgarh attempts were made to damage the railway bridge and wreak a mail train. It was said 'break up the bridge: the rule of the English has disappeared.'[43] The attempt to wreak No. 4 Down Mail at Bahadurgarh appeared to have been made because that train was known to be carrying a company of European wireless operators for Karachi.[44] On 15th April telegraph wires were also cut between Rohtak and Samar Gopalpur and at Gohana. At Sonepat a public meeting was held at Imambara. On 16th, at Rohtak a rumour spread about the rape of a weaver woman by soldiers which aroused excitement.[45] On 18tb April, at Kaithal the mob damaged the railway station. At Ambala the Sikh Pioneer Depot of 1/34 was burnt.[46] Similarly, on 20th April canal was cut near Jat High School, Rohtak.'[47]

Naturally, this explosive situation upset the Government. Sir Michael O'Dwyer, the Lieutenant-Governor of Punjab, felt angry about the happenings at Rohtak. In a letter to Lord Chelmford, the Viceroy of India, he wrote:[48] "Rohtak as a great Arya Samaj and also a great military district is reported very shocking though we have a staunch party of loyalists there,' consequently immediate increase in the police force was done. Special police guards were posted at all the important sites.[49] People were harassed by the bureaucracy. They were compelled for the *Thikri Pehra* (Patrolling Duty) for the protection of the telegraphs and the Railways. A local Defence Scheme was prepared at Rohtak in case of disturbances. Certain other precautionary measures were adopted. A sixteen-seated motor bus was obtained to ensure the mobility of the troops at Rohtak at any lime.[50] An armoured train was got together by the General Officer Commanding, Delhi Brigade and used for a journey to Bahadurgarh to demoralize the people.[51] An aeroplane hovered over Rohtak, Sampla, Bahadurgarh, Sonepat and Gunaur on 22nd April to terrorise the people.[52]

People of Haryana resisted at various places. People of Sanghi Kalan and Khadwali in Rohtak displayed boldness. Even Chaudhary Lal Chand of Rohtak confessed his inability to join the Government in a loyal manifesto or to issue one in his own name.[53] Ch. Peru Singh, Tek Ram, Abdul Aziz and Sagar Chand were arrested under Defence of India Rules. The Seditions Meetings Act was also extended to the entire region. Lala Kanshi Ram, Banwari Lal, Lala Munshi Ram, Lala Jwala Prasad, Lala Inder Sen were also arrested. In Gohana, Mulana Abdul Aziz was also arrested and sent to Lahore Central Jail for his critical views. Loyalists were offered rewards to repress the agitation at several places.

To sum up it can be said that the Rowlatt Bills' agitation was perhaps the first all India agitation which marked not only the beginning of the Gandhian struggle in this region but also widened and deepened the current of nationalism. Opposition to the Rowlatt Bills laid the foundation of an agitation, the intensity of which was unparalleled in the recent years.

The Khilafat Movement

The Khilafat[54] was a protest movement of the Indian Muslim against the hostile attitude of the Allies, particularly of the 'British Government, towards the Sultan of Turkey, whom they considered as the Khalifa (the spiritual leader). The Balkan Wars of 1912-13 made ample manifestation of the hostile British attitude towards Turkey. It was feared that the Sultan of Turkey would be completely deprived of all the authority after the war.

Maulana abdul Kalam Azad, Dr. M.A. Ansari, Dr. Saif-ud-Din Kitchlew, Maulvi Abdul Bari of Lucknow, Hakim Ajmal

Khan, the Ali-brothers—Mohammad Ali and Shaukat Ali and Dr. Syed Mahmud were the prominent leaders of the Khilafat movement. Its main object were the preservation of the Khilafat and maintaining the integrity of the Turkish empire.

As regards Haryana, the Khilafat Movement found some footing. In Haryana Abdul Rashid and Ghulam Beg Naurang, the pleaders, Khan Abdul Ghaffar Khan, a landlord, Hanif Khan and Hakim Shamim Ullah, businessmen in Ambala District, legullah and Sufi Iqbal, landlords, Maulana Usmani and Sanaunual Usmani, lambardars in Karnal District; Abdul Ghani Dar, a leading businessman of Ghasere, Mohhammed Yasu Khan, a landlord, Yakul Khan, an ex-Jamadar and a businessman of Palwal in Gurgaon District; Bakshi Ahmed Khan, a Hakim of Jhajjar, Zaman Ali, Haji Aladin, businessmen of Rohtak, Abdul Aziz, a shopkeeper of Gohana, Maulvi Mulhadan and Khair Mohemmed Khan, businessmen of Jhajjar Mohammed Shafi, a businessman of Bahadurgarh, Habibul Khan of Talao, and Maulvi Abdur Ghafar a landlord, Jan Mohammed, a member of Municipal Committee, Rohtak, Mustaq Hussain, leading lawyer in Rohtak District and Muhammed Usmani, a big business man of Bhiwani, Nazi Beg Muhammed Ismail and Nadir Khan, landlords of Hissar were the prominent leaders.[55] The Khilafat Committees with local leaders were formed in all the foremost districts and tehsils.[56]

After Amritsar Session of the Congress in 1919, the Khilafat Manifesto was issued in January 1920. Gandhi in his own way saw an opportunity of uniting Hindus and Muslims over the Khilafat cause. He gave enormous help to strengthen the cause of the Muslims. On 19th March 1920, the Khalifa Day was observed throughout the Haryana.

In April 1920, Pandit Neki Ram Sharma along with Lajpat Rai toured Hissar, Bhiwani and Rohtak and supported the movement.[57] In June Neki Ram Sharma addressed the public at Bhiwani in which he condemned the betrayal on the part of the Government.[58]

As a resuit of the movement, the agitation became intense in the rural areas also. The word 'Khilafat' was taken to mean 'against or opposed to' and Muslims took its meaning as opposed to the Government,[59] while officially it was understood as 'Khuli-Afat' (open revolt). The Government tried to subdue the movement. Loyalists were encouraged. A loyalist organisation entitled Kharkhuwa Majlis was established with its branches at Bhiwani, Rohtak, Gurgaon and Karnal. But this osganisation had little impact on the people.[60]

The Government also tried to suppress the movement by arresting all important leaders.[61] Persons from outside were not allowed to meet the Khalifat leaders in the Jail. Even Gandhi and Ali-brothers were not allowed to see them.[62] Public meetings were banned.

But with the expulsion of the Khalifa from Turkey in 1923, the Khilafat movement also began to lose its influence in India.[63]

The Non-Cooperation Movement

Along with the discontent caused due to the Punjab atrocities and dissatisfaction over the peace terms offered to Turkey, came the Report of the Disorders Inquiry Committee on 26th May, 1920. It had completely shaken the faith and confidence of the elite in the promises of the British Government of India. At a meeting of the Khalifat leaders in Delhi in November 1919, Gandhi first spoke of non-cooperation.[64] In the Gujarat Provincial Conference, Gandhi brought forward a resolution on Non-cooperation which was passed. The most vital aspects of the Non-cooperation Movement was the boycott of foreign cloth, legislature, law courts and educational institutions and renunciation of royal titles. On August 1, 1920 he warned Lord Chelmsford about his launching the Non-cooperation campaign and surrendered as a protest his decorations and titles of the Kaiser-i-Hind, the Zulu-War Medal and the Boer War Medal.[65] In September 1920, in a special Congress Session at Calcutta, Gandhi's resolution on Non-Violent-Non-cooperation was adopted by 1855 against 873 votes.[66]

Haryana witnessed the increasing tide of Non-cooperation. Firstly, the programme of mass mobilisation was made. Extensive tours of all India and provincial and regional level leaders were arranged. Propaganda committees were established at many places. Local leaders like Shri Ram Sharma, Ram Rup, Sham Lal, Daulat Ram Gupta toured Rohtak District.[67] Similarly Pandit Neki Ram Sharma, Duni Chand, Sham Lal, K.A. Desai visited Hissar, Ambala and Karnal districts.[68]

Then, extensive efforts for the establishment of the Congress committees was made for the first time in Haryana. In Rohtak Hissar, Gurgaon, Ambala and Karnal districts a number of the

Congress committees were established and their membership ran into thousands.

The Non-cooperation Movement in Haryana was launched at public meeting at Rohtak on 8th October 1920 wbich was attended by Gandhi along with Ali-brothers.[69] On 22nd October, the first Ambala Divisional Conference was held at Bhiwani It was presided over by Lala Murli Dhar and Gandhi was the chief guest. Ali Brothers, Maulana Abul Kalam Azad, Swami Satya Dev also attended the conference. Gandhi for the first time called the British Government as 'stantic Government.' He appealed the audience for the boycott of courts, services, schools, titles and the adoption of *Khaddar*.[70] Gandhi's visit to Haryana left a profound impact. His procession in Bhiwani was called as 'a march of democracy in a backward rural city.'[71]

At Rohtak District Conference was also held on 6-8 Nov. to pass a Non-cooperation resolution.[72] It was attended by Pandit Rambhuj Datta, Lala Lajpat Rai and Swami Satya Dev. One of the ugly events that happened in the Conference was that when the Non-cooperation pledge was to be taken by the audience, Chaudhary Chhotu Ram, a prominent Jat leader of Haryana, opposed it.[73] He vehementally criticised the non-payment of taxes and reuniciation of the titles, etc.[74] Molar Singh, the Editor of the *Jat Gazette* also supported Ch. Chhotu Ram, when K.A. Desai and Neki Ram Sharma tried to convince them, they were shouted down with the cry, 'O Pandit shut up. This is not Bhiwani.'[75] Consequently, Pandit Rambhuj Datta postponed the conference for the next day. Next day, the resolution was passed but the Congress lost the support of a great Jat leader. In fact, it was a great set back to the Congress in Haryana.

The programme of the boycott of Government aided institutions soon brought cessation of work in most of the Government-aided educational institutions. Gandhi's visit to Haryana stirred unrest among the student community.[76] Eighteen students left the Bahadurgarh High School and joined the National High School, Rohtak.[77] Gandhi also went to Kalanaur and Rohtak. He visited the Jat High School, Rohtak which had been lately 'nationalised.'[78] In thepresence of nearly 25,000 persons, the foundation stone of the Vaish High School, Rohtak, laid.[79] Ch. Chhotu Ram started a new Jat Heroes Memorial High School at Rohtak. He called the Movement as 'improper and a *chaal* (fraud) of Mahatma Gandhi.'[80] In Karnal and Ambala the boycott of schools and colleges could not be successful. In fact, the whole of the Punjab could not become a strong hold of the movement due to the boycott of educational institutions.

As regards the withdrawal of the candidates for election to the Reformed councils, which were to be held in November, 1920, the leaders of public opinon persuaded the educated classes not to enter councils till the wrong was redressed.[81] Pandit Neki Ram Sharma toured Haryana and tried to mobilize the people on this issue. He went to Sirsa, Bhiwani and Hissar and addressed the public meetings.[82] A number of vakils with- drew themselves from the Council's candidatures.[83] Lala Duni Chand, Vakil High Court, Ambala City withdrew himself for the Council's candidatures.[84] Similarly, Sham Lal, Jugal Kishore, Sheoran Dass, K.A. Desai, Harnam Singh and some others withdrew their candidatures for the Council election.[85]

So far as the boycott of the British court is concerned, some of the leading lawyers gave up their legal practice. Lala Sham Nath of Hissar gave up his practice for a year,[86] Lala Duni Chand, Shahjada Ram and Lala Tara Chand also gave up their practices. Great interest was shown for the establishment of *Panchayats*. In Bhiwani, a Rashtriya Nayalaya (National Court) was also established.[88] In the above court, six branches were opened and two appellate courts were also established.[89]

As to the renunciation of the titles only a small number of title holders had responded to the call. Lala Murli Dhar, the great old man of Punjab, renounced his title of "Rai Sahib', after the Jallianwala Bagh tragedy.[90] Mirza Nazir Beg, Ganpat Rai, Gokal Chand and Sukh Das from Bhiwani surrendered their Kurshi Nashinia, medals and certificates.[91] In Ambala, Hissar and Rohtak districts many *lambardars* and *Zaildars* had given up their posts.[92]

One of the remarkable aspects of the Non-cooperation Movement was the propagation of the *Swadeshi* and the boycott of foreign cloth. Gandhi toured the region also and appealed for a complete boycott of foreign clothes at any cost.[93] In Dehati Conference, Bhiwani, Gandhi declared, 'Give me Khaddar, I will give you Swaraj'.[94] A Khaddi procession was taken out in Rohtak on 1st August 1921.[95] Similar big processions were arranged advocating the case of Swadeshi at several places. At various places, the cloth merchants decided to sell only the *swadeshi* cloth.

In Sirsa, the businesmen resolved not to import the foreign cloth.[96] In Ambala a party of Congress volunteers approached nearly 60 cloth dealers of whom 45 agreed to boycott foreign cloth and gave their signatures and promises not to give fresh orders till the end of December.[97] The Muslims of Hansi numbering 7000, decided to boycott foreign cloth.[98] In Karnal a Khadi exhibition was arranged and prizes were distributed to Khadi manufacturers.[99] At Bhiwani, the cloth-contractors boycotted those cloth-dealers who did not accept the principle for the boycott of foreign cloth.[100] In Rewari, a wedding ceremony was postponed owing to the refusal of the bridegroom to marry the bridge clad in foreign fineries.[101]

In fact, Khaddi became the symbol of patriotism. When Abdul Rashid and Lala Duni Chand released from the jail, they were welcomed by erecting 40 gates of Khaddar. One of the gates was of *charkha,* in which the flowers of *Khaddar* was bestowed on them.[102] Even the welcome address was also printed on Khaddar.[103]

The people also made substantial contribution to Tilak Swaraj Fund. At Rural Conference Bhiwani, held on 15th February, 1921, Gandhi got ₹ 60,000 against this.[104] Even Hissar Municipal Committee offered a donation of ₹ 100 despite official objection.

Picketing of liquor shops was also made enthusiastically. At Rohtak and Karnal the picketing took place and no bidder could be found at the time of annual auctions.[105] At Ambala, the picketers were manhandled by police,[106] and were imprisoned for three months for not allowing the auction bidding.[107] As a protest against the police high-handedness, the Jhajjar Congress Committee decided to picket the octroi posts.[108] Shri Ram Sharma of Jhajjar was arrested. At the Municipal Committee the Union Jack was torn and the national flag was hoisted. Some typical events also occurred. For example, in Sirsa, the people plastered the face of King Edward's Statute. They also took over a procession with two donkeys in European fashion to represent one English man and a woman.[109] In Rohtak, a playcard in a neck of dog was hanged on which it was written 'I am an Englishman.'[110]

Due to all these activities, even Lord Reading, the then Viceroy of India, admitted in December, 1921 that the Government was puzzled and perplexed.[111] Now the local Government adopted repressive measures. Seditious meetings Act was enforced. Certain leading papers were prosecuted. Individual restrictions were imposed. Bakshi Ram Krishan of Hissar, Pandit Neki Ram

Sharma, Shri Luxmi Narayan, Sham Lal of Hissar, Shri Ram Sharma of Jhajjar, Murli Dhar Lala Murli Dhar, Lala Duni Chand and Lala Goverdhan Das were arrested. Anti-non-cooperation meetings were arranged by the officials at several places,[112] in which *jihuzars*,[113] the members of the Aman Sabhas and Rajbhagat Sabha took part.[114]

Unfortunately, violence erupted at Chauri Chora in Gorakhpur District, in which 22 policemen were murdered by a violent mob on the 5th February 1922. Gandhi declared the suspension of the Movement and consequently on February 12, the movement was withdrawn. Gandhi was criticized by the prominent leaders and it was considered a 'blunder' on his part.

Though the Movement failed, yet it left its imprint on the growth of India's struggle for freedom. Perhaps the period during 1920-21 'proved the worst moment for Britain's imperial rulers in India in the ninety years between the Mutiny and 1942.'[115] In Haryana, the impact of Non-Cooperation Movement was intensive and it had succeeded in creating an atmosphere of hostility against the Government.[116] It widened the gulf between the Government and the masses. Secondly, the Congress organisation for the first time in history was set up in Haryana. Pandit Neki Ram Sharma and Lala Deshbandhu Gupta played a dynamic role in establishing its branches throughout Haryana.[117] During the period 80 Congress committees were established in Rohtak District, 30 in Hissar, 20 in Gurgaon, and 40 each in Ambala and Karnal.

The Outbursts of Communal Hatred

One of the major casualties due to the termination of the Non-Cooperation Movement by Gandhi, was the Hindu-Muslim unity. The people of Haryana also engaged themselves in local trivialities and Hindu-Muslim conflicts.

In July 1923, a central Jamiat-i-Tabligh-ul-Islam was formed with headquarters at Ambala and Syed Bhik Narang, a leading vakil of Ambala was appointed its organisational Secretary.[118] The Khilafat leaders had encouraged the Muslims to a 'new and more dynamic programme,'[119] for the unity of the whole community. The Tanzim (organisation) and Tabligh (Conversion) Movement became popular. Similarly, among the Hindus the *Shuddi* and *Sangathan* movement gained momentum. Swami Sharddhanand took leading part in the latter.

There were some other factors which stirred the communal feelings. One of the factors had been the formation of the legislative council and local bodies on the basis of a separate electorate. The result had been the formation of the commuanl groups which were constantly at loggerheads with each other. The proposal of the redistribution of seats and the extension of communal representation in local bodies by Mian-Fazl-i-Husain, the then Education Minister of Punjab, further excited communal passions. The Muslims up to 1922 had never demanded more seats in municipalities. Consequently, it led to communal strife. The non-Muslims of the Municipal Council at Ambala resigned.[120]

Secondly, the economic domination of the Hindu over the Muslim gave an impression to the Muslim that he was in danger. 'The fall in prices which occurred in the middle of 1922 left him with a heavy burden of debt and with little means to repay.'[121] Perhaps this economic factor was vital in the communal outbreaks.[122] Monev-lenders Bill, latter known as, Borrowed Protection Bill' was widely opposed by the Hindus and it further created a gulf between the rural and urban classes.[123]

Another factor was the political position of various groups. The All India Congress lost its hold after the failure of the Non-cooperation Movement. The Muslim League was also not popular. In 1926 parties like the Hindu Sabha and Punjab Swaraksha Sabha gained more strength than the Congress itself.

As a result of the growing communal consciousness a series of communal riots took place in Haryana also. In August, riots occurred in Panipat. The cause of the disturbances was Muslim objection to 'Arti' (worship) being performed in Hindu temples while the call for prayer 'Azan' was being made in the mosques.[124] Rumours that the Muslims intended sacrificing cows on a large scale at the Bakr-id festival further increased the tension.[125] The Mahabir Dal[126] and of the Ali Ghol[127] were formed ostensibly for encouraging the physical culture. In August 1925 the trouble again rose in Panipat, due to strained relations between the Hindus and the Muslims.[128] The years of 1926 and 1927 also witnessed strife at Ambala, Karnal and Rohtak. Swami Sharddhanand was assaulted on 23rd December 1926. In 1928 two Hindu-Muslim riots occurred, one on Bakr-id in a village of Ambala District in which 10 people Were killed and 9 injured and the other at Softa village of Gurgaon District in which 14 persons were killed and 33 injured.[129]

In short, from 1923 to 1928 nearly 14 riots took place in Haryana. In the series of riots, Panipat had the highest *i.e.* 4 riots, perhaps it was due to the fact that here the Muslims were in majority, Population of the Muslims was 19,975 while that of the Hindus was only 6,561.

The communal riots shocked Gandhi, but the twenty-one days fast, the Unity Conference I and the establishment of a Central National Panchayat produced no tangible results. In fact, the riots created a certain degree of aloofness in so far as her internal affairs[130] were concerned and matters of vital importance were relegated to the background.

Constitutional Reforms in Practice

While the communal conflicts adversely affected the political and constitutional developments in the country, the Reforms were introduced in an atmosphere of distrust and bitterness, engendered by the non-cooperation and accentuated by the Jallianwala Bagh tragedy. Most of the leaders refrained from participating in the elections.

The first Reformed Punjab Council constituted in 1921, had (besides 23 nominated officials and non-officials) 71 elected members, of whom 35 were Muslims, 15 Sikhs and 21 Hindus.

The first enlarged Punjab Council on the whole represented 'the more moderate current of political opinion in Punjab',[131] and was by 'no means an extremist body',[132] it was 'definitely loyal'.[133] Most of the elected members were without specific party. The residential qualifications brought mainly the land proprietors from the rural constituencies. The urban members were mostly lawyers, with a sprinkling of commercial and retired officers.[134] Mian Fazl-i-Husain formed a party of his own which came to be known as the Rural Bloc, but was later called the Rural Party. It was mainly 'agriculturist' and its policy was pro-British, and anti-urbanite Hindus and Sikhs.[135] Out of the elected members, one fourth did not know English and some were illiterate.[136]

During this period due to the communal tensions, the Council could not make any progress. In the end of 1923, Lala Harkishan, the then Minister of Agriculture, had resigned due to the undue interference of the Government of India in the Finance

Department and his appearance in Sir Sankaran Nair's case as witness in O'Dwyer vs Nair.[137] Now Rai Bahadur Chaudhry Lal Chand, a rural Hindu, was selected as Minister of Agriculture. He was later found guilty of adopting corrupt practices and was compelled to resign.[138]

The election of the Second Reformed Council witnessed a dear clash between the Congress and the Unionists Party. It also showed a marked political advance in the party-system. For the first time in the history of Punjab an election manifesto was brought out.[139] The abolition of residential qualifications provided a wider field of selection to rural constituencies. This time the electorate showed greater interest than before in exercising their franchise. During the elections of 1920 the percentage of votes was low (32%) owing to the non-cooperation movement but in the general election of 1923, 49% of the voters recorded their votes.[140] Out of total 71 elected members, 9 were selected from Haryana. The party position in the Punjab Legislative Council in 1923 was as follow:

Name of the Party of Group	*Seats won from Punjab*	*Seats won from Haryana*	*Total*
Swarajists Moderates	7	2	9
(including unionists)	31	7	38
Independents	11	—	11
Loyalists	—	—	—
Liberals Shiromani Gurudwara	—	—	—
Prabandhak Committee	10	—	10
Khilafatists	3	—	3
Total	62	9	71

A significant aspect of the election was the entry of the Swarajist Party. In Punjab, the educated opinion in the Congress appeared in favour of the Swarajist party.[141] By the efforts of C.R. Das and Motilal Nehru, a branch of the Swaraj Party was established in Punjab on the 9th April 1923.[142] Lala Duni Chaud of Ambala, a member of the Provincial Committee of Swaraj party played a significant role. Out of the 9 Swarajist seats won in the Punjab Legislative Council, two were from Haryana. These were begged by Lala Duni Chand of Ambala and Lala Sham Lal of Hissar. All the other seven seats from Haryana were won by the Unionists. They were Mohammad Shafi Ali Khan (Ambala), Ganga Ram (Ambala), Duli Chand (Karnal), Pohap Singh (Gurgaon), Sahib

Dad Khan (Gurgaon), Chhotu Ram (Rohtak) and Lal Chand (Rohtak). Chhotu Ram was now appointed as Minister by the Lieutenant-Governor, Sir Malcolm Hailey.

The elections to the third new Council were held in November 1926. The Congress sustained severe reverses[143] and the main cause of these reverses was the resignation of Lajpat Rai from the membership of the Swarajist party,[144] and the death of C.R. Das. Secondly the conditions imposed on the members of the-Congress that they should wear *Khaddar* did not appeal to all Congressmen.[145] Thirdly, the internal conflicts of the Congressmen came into forefront. Pandit Madan Mohan Malaviya and Lajpat Rai formed a new independent Congress Party which was opposed to the aya-gaya (coming and going) policy of the Swarajist party and also the Congress party on the communal questions.[146] Pt. Neki Ram Sharma undertook an extensive tour of Haryana during the election days of Oct-Nov. 1926 in favour of the Independent Party. Lajpat Rai and Pt. Madan Mohan Malaviya also visited several places in Haryana to oppose the Swarajist candidates.

The Congress Swaraj Party secured only 3 seats as against 9 in 1923.[147] The only important group which played the dominating role in the Punjab legislative Council was the Unionist party, previously the Rural party, headed by Mian Fazl-i-Husain and Chaudhary Chhotu Ram. Its basic object was to assist and encourage the backward areas and backward communities. But it could not have until now sufficient hold in Haryana. It secured only four seats. Sir Rahim Baksh Maulvi (Ambala), Duli Chand (Karnal), Yasin Khan (Gurgaon) and Ch. Chhotu Ram (Rohtak) were elected on its tickets. Out of the five remaining seats in Haryana, two were won by the Independent-Congress party. The successful candidates were Mr. Thakur Das (Ambala) and Chhaju Ram (Hissar). A new feature of the election was the success of the Hindu Sabha in Haryana. It secured two seats, Ganga Ram (Ambala) and Balbir Singh (Gurgaon) were elected on its tickets. One seat had gone to the Swarajists, their candidate Baldev Singh was elected from Rohtak.

In nutshell, the frequent changes in the political set up show that in Haryana very little political advancement took place. Perhaps it was conceived more on communal or caste bases than on political opinion.

Boycott of the Simon Commission

There was a lull in the political environment of the country. Every where confusion and depression was prevailing due to the communal riots. At this juncture, keeping in view the forthcoming elections, the conservative Prime Minister announced the appointment of Simon Commission on November 8, 1927. In fact, according to the section 84 of the Act of 1919, it was to be appointed in 1929. As it was purely whitemen commission and no Indian was included, practically all the parties decided to boycott the Commission.[149]

The All India Congress met at Madras in 1927 and passed the resolution relating to the boycott of Simon Commission.[150] The All India Muslim League, the Khilafat leaders and even the National Liberal Federation also decided to boycott the Commission. Consequently, it was greeted everywhere with black flags and the slogans like 'Simon go back'.

In Haryana numerous meetings were held for boycotting and condemning the appointment of the Commission. Important meetings were held at Bhiwani, Gurgaon, Jagadhari, Rohtak and Jhajjar and resolutions were passed against this appointment.

Meanwhile, on 30th October 1928, an incident occurred at Lahore, which excited popular feelings. Lala Lajpat Rai was assaulted by the police when he was leading a peaceful procession, which resulted into Lajpat Rai's death. His death on the 17th November 1928 created a widespread resentment throughout the country. Gandhi said that Lalaji's demise means the setting of a great planet from India's solar system.[151] Pt. Neki Ram Sharma held the Commission responsible for Lala Lajpat Rai's death.[152] His death was considered a great challenge and a big national insult. The people felt humbled and insulted and the youth pledged for the revenge.

Anyhow, the boycott of the Simon Commission proved to be a uniting bond of the scattered political elements in the country. Lajpat Rai's death stirred an intense revolutionary mentality among the youth of the country.[153]

The Revolutionary Activities: the Naujawan Bharat Sabha and the Kisan Party

Then followed the formation of the Naujwan Bharat Sabha, (Indian Youth Association) the prime youth organisation of Punjab and Haryana. It was anti-British and pro-socialist association. It was formed in Lahore in March 1926 by Dr. Satyapal.[154]

Its prominent members were Bhagwati Charan, Yash Pal, Sukh Dev and Jai Chand Vidyalankar. In the beginning, the activities of the Sabha comprised of debates on moral, literary and social subjects, lectures on Swadeshi goods, unity, plain living, physical fitness, the Indian culture and civilization.[155] For its membership, every person was made to sign a pledge that he would place the interest of his country above those of his community.[156] In April 1928, its aims were modified as follows:[157]

1. To establish a complete independent Republic of the labourers and peasants of the whole of India.
2. To infuse a spirit of patriotism into the hearts of the Youth of the country in order to establish a United Indian Nation.
3. To express sympathy with, and to assist the economic, industrial and social movements which, while being free from communal sentiment, are intended to take us nearer to our ideal, namely the establishment of a complete independent republic of labourers and peasants.
4. To organise the labourers and peasants.

In Haryana its branches were established in Ambala, Karnal, Rohtak and Hissar districts.[158] Some of the prominent leaders of Naujawan Bharat Sabha in Haryana[159] were Gopal Das, Rajendra Singh and Sardar Singh in Ambala; Dev Raj in Karnal; Lachman Das, Mange Ram Vats, Chandu Lal, Murari Lal, Ram Saran Das, Atma Nand and Daulat Ram Gupta in Rohtak: and Durga Das Gupta, Bhagwan Das Gautam, Lekh Ram, Thakur Shish, Pal Singh, Radha Krishan Verma, K.A. Desai, Banwari Lal Hari Singh, Mohan Chand, Chhote Lal and Bhagwati Swarup in Hissar. Anyhow, its activities in Haryana were limited. It could not become as significant as it was in Punjab. Perhaps, it was due to its limited membership, lack of dashing leadership, lack of funds and lack of proper organization.[160] Similarly, the Socialist leanings of the Sabha could not gather more momentum in Haryana. It aroused only one or two agrarian agitations in 1928[161] but could not move the peasants. Perhaps the Sabha had only one village branch in Ambala[162] and mainly it was confined to the cities and middle class people.[163] In fact, its leaders in Haryana were more or less pro-Congress.

The Government also vigorously tried to suppress the movement. The Sabha was declared unlawful association.[164] All the offices of Naujawan Sabha were searched and confiscated by the Government.[165] Some arrests were also made at different places, and its members were ill-treated in the Jails.[166]

Though the Sabha left no vital mark in Haryana yet it played a significant role in the political advancement during 1926-1929 by spreading anti-British movements and revolutionary ideas among the youth. In Haryana, a number of youth organisations started in different names like Naujawan Hindu Sabha at Hissar and Ambala,[167] Youth League at Rohtak[168] and Bal Bharat Sabha at Mandi Dabwali.[169]

Along with Naujawan Sabha other important revolutionary group was known as Kirti Kisan Party. It owes its origin from the Gurmukhi paper 'Kirti' in Feb. 1926 by Santokh Singh, an Indian revolutionary in U.S.A. who was tried in San Francisco conspiracy case. Perhaps it was the first Punjabi paper defending the Interest of the working class. The paper believed in Marxist ideology and the revolutionary methods. In April 1928 at Amritsar the Kirti-Kisan Party was formed to organise the workers and peasants. Sohan Singh Josh and M.A. Majid were elected its Secretary and the Joint Secretary respectively.[170] In its second Conference at Lyallpur in Sept. 1928, it detemined to fight against *begar* and sought reduction in taxes and land revenue.[171] One of its branches suggested the boycott of the 'Zamindra League' started by Chhotu Ram.[172] Its third Conference was held at Rohtak on 10 March 1928 in which Jawaharlal Nehru also participated.[173] Now it changed its name as Worker's and Peasant's Party in place of Kirti Kisan Party. Like the Naujawan Sabha, the organisation was suppressed by the repressive measures of the government. Its impact in Haryana region seems to be nominal and thereafter in April 1934 it stimulated Hissar Kisan Sabha to a campaign against the payments of rent in kind, in place of cash to the landlords.[174]

The Bomb incident in the Central Assembly at New Delhi on April 8, 1929 again gave new impetus to the youth of the country. These bombs had been thrown by Bhagat Singh and Batukesashwar Datta. Both of them surrendered themselves. A number of arrests were also made. Later their moving statements and hunger strikes stirred the patriotic feelings throughout the country. Death of Jatinder Nath on Ist October 1929 on the 63rd day of his fast caused great resentment. In fact it strengthened a spirit of patriotism and wave of political consciousness in the country.

Congress Session at Lahore 1929

With the sporadic revolutionary activities, the year 1929 witnessed the year with political and industrial unrest, the economic depression and discontent. The year also witnessed with the hectic activities of the Congress. In Haryana on 8-9th March 1929. Punjab Provincial Political Conference was held a:t Rohtak,[175] which was attended by Motilal Nehru, and Jawaharlal Nehru. Dr. Satyapal presided over the Session. In the Conference several significant resolutions[176] on Nehru Report, remission of Land revenue due to the failure of crops etc. were passed. A process of re-establishing a net work of the Congress Committee again picked up. New Congress committees were formed at Rohtak, Hissar, Karnat and Ambala.[177] In Gurgaon it could not gain any success.

So with the new energies inculcated by the establishment of the Congress Committees, the Congress session at Lahore was held in 1929. In this session for the first time the resolution of the declaration of *Puran Swaraj* (Complete independence) was assed. It was pledged to carryout the Congress instructions issued from time to time for the purpose of establishing *Puran* Swaraj.[178] It urged the Congressmen to resign their seats in the supreme and provincial legislature and not to stand for future elections, It was also resolved not to participate in the coming Round Table Conference. Other important resolutions concerned the fundamental rights of Indian states, the Communal question and the state of Indians in East Africa. In fact, the Lahore session of the Congress produced new energies in the national movement and with it emerged the youth leadership in the country.

NOTES

1. J.K. Majumdar: *Indian Speeches and Documents on British Policy,* (Calcutta, 1937), p, 186; C.F. Andrews and Girija Mookerji: *op. cit.*, p. 242.
2. See statement of Mr. R.C. Bolster, the Deputy Commissioner, Rohtak, Vide *The Disorders Inquiry Committee, Evidence,* Vol. V, p. 242.
3. *Ibid.*
4. See Sir C. Sankaran Nair: *An Autobiography,* (Madras, 1966), p. 359.
5. For detail consult the *Proceedings of the Imperial Legislative Council,* Vol. LVII, (April 1918-March 1919).

6. *Ibid.*, p. 455.
7. *Ibid.*, p. 457.
8. *Ibid.*, p. 463.
9. *Ibid.*, p. 510.
10. *Ibid.*, p. 904.
11. *Ibid.*, p. 519.
12. *Ibid.*, p. 520.
13. *Ibid.*
14. *Ibid.*, p. 536.
15. *Ibid.*, p. 538.
16. Rajendra Prasad: *Autobiography*, (Bombay, 1957), p. 107.
17. M.K. Gandhi, *The Story of My Experiments with Truth*, p. 278.
18. *The Tribune*, 20-3-1919.
19. *Ibid.*, 16-2-1919.
20. *Ibid.*, 16-2-1919.
21. *Ibid.*, 4-3-1919.
22. R. Kumar (Ed.), *Essays on Gandhian Politics, The Rowlatt Satyagraha*, 1919, p. 208.
23. *Home Department* (*Political*), *Government of India, Proceedings*, 1920, F., 373.
24. *Ibid.*
25. See statement of Mr. H.K. Trevaskis, the Deputy Commissioner, Gurgaon, vide *The Disorders Inquiry Committee*, Vol. V., p. 242.
26. *Ibid.*
27. *Ibid.*
28. *Ibid.*, vide statement of Mr. R.C. Bolster, the Deputy Commissioner, Rohtak, p. 242.
29. *Ibid.*
30. *Ibid.*
31. *Ibid.*, p. 243.
32. *Ibid.*, vide statement of Mr. R.B. Whitehead, the Deputy Commissioner, Ambala, p. 244.
33. Jagdish Chander, *op. cit.*, p. 40.
34. *Home Department* (*Political B*), *Government of India, Proceedings, April 1920, Nos. 94-97*; M.M. Juneja: *op. cit.*, pp. 13-14.
35. *The Disorders Inquiry Committee, Evidence, Vol. V*, statement of Mr. R.C. Bolster, D.C. Rohtak, p. 243.
36. Shri Ram Sharma: *Haryana Ke Itihas*, p. 60.
37. *The Disorders Inquiry Committee*, Vol. V, p. 243.
38. *Home Department* (*Political B*), *Govt. of India, Proceedings May 1919, Nos. 141-147*; *See also* Balwan Singh Sulakhi: *Swami Shardhanand*, (Unpublished Thesis, Kurukshetra, University, 1978), p. 67; *The Disorders Inquiry Committee Evidence*, Vol., I, Delhi. See Swami Shardhanand Statement, p. 189.
39. *Home Department* (*Political B*), *Govt. of India, Proceedings*, May 1919, pp. 141-47.
40. *Home Department* (*Political B*), *Govt. of India, Proceedings*, May 1919, Nos. 268-273.

41. *M.R. Jayakar's Diary*, April 11, 1919.
42. *The Disorders Inquiry Committee, Vol. V*, statement of Mr. R.B. Whitehead, the D.C, Ambala, p. 244; *Home Department* (*Political B*) *Govt. India*, Nov. 1919, Nos. 133-137.
43. *Ibid.*
44. *Ibid.*, p 244.
45. *Ibid.*, p. 243 (statement of D.C., Rohtak)
46. *The Disorders Inquiry Committee, Evidence*, Vol. V, pp. 190-91, Vol. VI, p. 116.
47. *The Disorders Inquiry Committee, Evidence*, Vol. V, Statement of D.C., Rohtak, p. 243.
48. *Chelmsford Papers* 1919 Letter from Sir Michael O'Dwyer to Lord Chelmsford, April 21st, 1919, p. 337.
49. *The Disorders Inquiry Committee, Evidence*, Vol. VI, p. 116, 130-33, 147-8.
50. *Ibid.* Vol. V, statement of D.C. Rohtak, p. 243.
51. *Ibid.*
52. *Ibid.*
53. *Ibid.*, p. 244.
54. For detail *see* A.C. Niemeiji: *The Khilafat Movement in India* 1919-20, (Hague, 1972), pp. 69-98.
55. Jagdish Chander: *op. cit.*, pp. 56-57.
56. *The Tribune*, 23-3-1920.
57. *Ibid.*, 20-4-1920.
58. *Ibid.*, 22-6-1920; M.M. Juneja: *op. cit.*, p. 17.
59. J. Nehru: *Autobiography*, p. 69; D.G. Tandulkar; *op. cit.*, Vol. II, p. 34.
60. *Home Department* (*Political B*), *Govt. of India, May* 1920, No. 83.
61. *The Tribune*, 6-10-1920.
62. *Ibid.*, 10-10-1920.
63. *Home Department* (*Political B*), *Govt. of India*, Proceedings, 1924, 6/IX.
64. P.C. Ghosh: *Mahatma Gandhi as I Saw Him*, (Delhi, 1968), pp. 88 and 91.
65. D.C. Tandulkar: *op. cit.*, Vol. II, p. 1.
66. *The Collected Works of Mahatma Gandhi*, Vol. XVIII (Delhi), p. 260,
67. *The Tribune*, 27-2-1921, 12-6-1921 and 15-6-1921.
68. *Ibid.*, 12-6-1921, 15-6-1921.
69. *Home Department* (*Political B*), *Govt. of India, Proceedings*, Dec. 1920. Nos. 183-86, and K.W.
70. *The Collected Works of Mahatma Gandhi*, Vol. XVIII, p. 365.
71. *The Tribune*, 27-10-1920.
72. *Ibid.*, 5-11-1920.
73. *Ibid.*, 13-11-1920, H.L. Agnihotri and Shiva Lal Malik; *A Profile in Courage, A Biography of Ch. Chhotu Ram*, p. 20.
74. *Ibid.*
75. *Ibid.*
76. Algu Rai Shastri: *Lajpat Rai* (Prayag, 1957), p. 345.
77. *The Tribune*, 27-1-1921; S.C. Mittal: Haryana Men Ashayog Andolan, *Jan Sahitya*, August 1971, p. 46.

78. *The Tribune*, 19-2-1921.
79. *The Collected Works of Mahatma Gandhi*, Vol. XIX, p. 369; S.C. Mittal; Haryana Men Ashyog Andolan, *Jan Sahitya*, p. 46.
80. *The Jat Gazettee Rohtak*, 10th November 1920; *The Tribune*, 28-11-1920.
81. *The Tribune*, 16-10-1920.
82. *Ibid.*, 22-11-1920, 1-12-1920, 2-12-1920.
83. M.M. Juneja: *op. cit.*, p. 23.
84. *The Tribune*, 7-10-1920.
85. *Ibid.*, 28-10-1920.
86. *Ibid.*, 19-2-1921.
87. *Ibid.*, 24-5-1921.
88. *Ibid.*, 26-5-1921.
89. *Ibid.*
90. *Ibid.*, 17-9-1920.
91. *Ibid.*, 28-10-1920.
92. *Ibid.*, 26-5-1921
93. *Ibid.*, 19-2-1921; *The Collected Works of Mahatma Gandhi*, Vol. XVIII, pp. 337, 357-9.
94. *Home Department* (*Political*), *Govt. of India, Proceedings*, Dec. 1924, file No. 25.
95. *The Tribune*, 6-8-1921.
96. *Ibid.*, 27-8-1921.
97. *Ibid.*, 15-9-1921.
98. *Ibid.*, 29-7-1921.
99. *Ibid.*, 1-10-1921.
100. *Ibid.*, 20-1-1921.
101. *A.I.C.C. Papers*, Reports of the Work done by the Congress in Punjab, p. 145.
102. *The Tribune*, 17-8-1921.
103. *Ibid.*
104. *The Collected Works of Mahatma Gandhi, Vol. XVIII*, pp. 360-61.
105. *A.I.C.C. Papers*, Part I, p. 9.
106. *Ibid.*, pp. 19-25.
107. *Ibid.*, p. 9.
108. *Ibid.*, Pt. II, p. 27; *The Tribune*, 19-1-1922 and 8-2-1922.
109. *Home Department*. (*Political-B*) *Govt. of India, Proceedings*, Oct. 1921 p. 18.
110. *Ibid.*
111. J. Nehru: *An Autobiography*, pp. 70 and 87.
112. *The Tribune*, 11-6-1921
113. *Ibid.*, 12-6-1921.
114. *Ibid.*, 22-11-1921.
115. *See* D.A. Law: The Government of India and First Non-Cooperation Movement 1920-21, *Essays on Gandhi Politics* (Ed. R. Kumar).
116. *Punjab Legislative Council, Proceedings* (10th January, 1921), p. 51.
117. S.C. Mittal. *Haryana Men Ashayog* Andolan, *Jan Sahitya*, August 1971, p. 50.
118. *Home Department* (*Political*), *Govt. of India, Proceedings*, Sept. 1924, 6/1X.

119. *Ibid.*
120. *Home Department (Political), Govt. of India Proceedings,* July 1923, Feb. 25.
121. *Punjab Administration Report,* 1922-23, p. 3.
122. *Ibid.*
123. *The People,* 4-4-1926 and *The Tribune,* 20-11-1924.
124. *The Tribune* 29-8-1923.
125. *Home Department (Political), Govt. of India, Proceedings,* July 1923, p. 25.
126. *Home Department (Political), Govt. of India, Proceedings,* July 1923, F. 25.
127. *Home Department (Political), Govt. of India, Proceedings;* October, 1923-25.
128. *The Tribune,* 4-8-1925 and 15-8-1928.
129. *India in 1928-29,* pp. 3-4.
130. Duni Chand: *The Ulster of India,* pp. v-vi; R. Coupland: *The Constitutional Problem of India,* Part I, p. 41.
131. *Punjab Administrative Report 1922-23,* p. 17.
132. *Ibid.*
133. *Ibid.*
134. *Ibid.*
135. Khushwant Singh: *A History of the Sikhs,* Vol. II, p. 245.
136. *The Tribune,* 11-1-1921.
137. K.L. Gauba: *The Hon'ble Sir Shadi Lal,* p. 94.
138. *The Tribune,* 16-7-1924.
139. Azim Husain: *Mian-Fazl-i-Husain, A Political Biography,* p. 152.
140. *Punjab Administrative Report,* 1923-24, p. 7.
141. *Home Department (Political), Govt. of India,* 1923, Feb. 25.
142. *Ibid., The Tribune,* 11-4-1923.
143. *The Tribune,* 8-12-1926.
144. *Ibid.,* 1-9-1926 and 4-9-1926.
145. *Ibid.,* 18-6-1925.
146. V.C. Joshi: *Lajpat Rai—A Biographical Essay,* p. 42; *The Tribune,* 14-9-1926.
147. *The Tribune,* 8-12-1926.
148. Azim Husain: *op. cit.,* p. 155.
149. *The Tribune,* 5-2-1928.
150. *The People,* Vol. VI, Part I, 1928, p. 5.
151. *Ibid.,* Vol. VII, p. 321.
152. *A.I.C.C. Proceedings,* 1928, (Calcutta), p. 156.
153. D.G. Tandulkar; *op. cit.,* Vol. II, p. 335.
154. *Home Department (Political), Govt. of India,* April, 1928, p. 18.
155. *Ibid.,* 1930, File 130.
156. *Ibid.*
157. *Ibid.,* Virendra Sandhu: *Yugdrastra Bhagat Singh Aur Unke Mirtyunjay Purkhee,* p. 153; *see also* Bhagwan Josh: *Communist's Movement in Punjab,* (Dec. 1979), pp. 82-83.
158. *Home Department (Political)* Govt. of India, 1930, F. 130.
159. For detail *see* Jagdish Chander: *op. cit.,* p. 120.

160. *Home Department* (*Political*) *Govt. of India*, 1930, F. 130/K.W.
161. Bipin Chandra, *Nationalism and Colonialism in Modern India*, Delhi, 1969), p. 239.
162. *Ibid*., p. 13.
163. *Ibid*., 36 ff.
164. *Home Department* (*Political*), *Govt. of India*, 1930, F. 418 and K.W.
165. *Ibid*.
166. *The Tribune*, 24-12-1930.
167. *Ibid*., 12-3-1931.
168. *Ibid*., 4-9-1930.
169. *Ibid*.
170. Bhagwan Josh: *op. cit*., p. 92.
171. *Ibid*. p. 93.
172. *Ibid*.
173. *Ibid*., p. 90.
174. *Ibid*., p. 102.
175. *The Tribune*, 10-3-1929.
176. *Ibid*., 13-3-1929
177. *Ibid*., 18-5-1929, 2-10-1929.
178. *A.I.C.C. File No. 4-136-1930*. Part II, pp. 559-60.

7

Puran Swaraj: From Resolution to Achievement (1930-1947)

The Civil Disobedience Movement (1930-34)

The year 1930 witnessed the celebration of the complete Independene Day' on Sunday, the 26th January throughout the country. In this Day determination of 'Puran Swaraj' was made. Resolutions were passed and the pledges were taken. On 14-16th February 1930, the Congress Working Committee passed the Civil Disobedience Resolution at Sabarmati and Gandhi was given the right to guide the movement. On 2nd March, Gandhi warned the Viceroy about the launching of the *Satyagraha*.[1] In March 1930 Gandhi undertook the historical Dandi March with 78 *Satyagrahis* hailing from various regions including Haryana. It was called by Motilal Nehru as the historic March of 'Ramchandra to Lanka'[2] or like the exodus of the Israelites under Moses[3] by P. C. Roy, or Napoleon's march to Paris on his return from Elba of Mussolini's march to Rome when he wanted to seize political power.[4] On 6th April, a countrywide Civil Disobedience Movement was started. Gandhi broke the Salt Law at Aat on 8th April.

In Haryana public meetings were held. Resolutions for the celebration of complete independence were passed. Prominent leaders of national and provincial stature like M. M. Malaviya, Gopi Chand Bhargava, Abdur Ghaffar, Suraj Bhan visited various places.[5] Salt laws were broken. For example, at Rewari illicit salt was prepared and auctioned for ₹ 10312,[6] A packet of salt was purchased by a twelve years old girl for ₹ 60, which was her total saving at the rate of two pies a day.[7] At Hissar on the 13th April, salt was manufacturee.[8] In Bhiwani it was prepared in iron pans.[9] Similarly, salt laws were broken at Rohtak[10] and Ambala[11] on 10th and 25th April respectively. Along with the illegal manufacture of salt, the boycott of foreign clothes were made. Picketing was made on the shops which were selling foreign cloth at Sirsa, Abdulapur, Abdul Masjid.[12] The cloth dealers of Rohtak, Bhiwani and Ambala pledged not to import foreign cloth.[13] The foreign sugar and vegetable ghee was also boycotted.

Thirdly, the *Swadeshi* or *Khaddar* was propagated. At Ambala nearly 5,000 people pledged to wear *Khaddar*.[14] Some women started picketing at temples and allowed entry to only those persons who were in *Khaddar*.[15]

Fourthly, picketing of liquor shops also took place. It was to reduce the consumption of liquor and to decrease the excise duty.[16] At Rohtak and Ambala liquor shops were picketed.[17] A liquor vender was socially boycotted and his house was surrounded by the mob on 8th August.[18]

Fifthly, some futile efforts were made for boycotting the educational institutions. But in Haryana it could not succeed as the proposal was opposed by the parents and guardians.

Sixthly, similarly the picketing of law courts proved unsuccessful.

Seventhly, some attempts were made at picketing polling booths for the election to the Assembly and Council at Rohtak. But the proposal was opposed by the Jats of Rohtak.[19] In Ambala District some *Banias* abstained from voting.[20]

Lastly, a significant feature of the Civil Disobedience Movement was against the high rent. The Kisans of Skinner Estate (consisting of 15 villages) formed a Kisan Sabha in January 1929 under the leadership of Pt. Neki Ram Sharma of Bhiwani and Lajpat Rai of Alakhpura. The peasants refused to pay taxes. Neki Ram Sharma voiced against the *Begar*. Soon the two Skinners compromised with the peasants and reduced the land revenue.

The Government of India did not pay much attention towards the Civil Disobedience Movement in the beginning. But soon it realized its gravity. Now the Government adopted the coercive methods. Leaders were arrested. There was firing and lathi charge in prominent cities and towns. Processions and public meetings were banned. The Press Act of 1910 was again revived by the Viceroy. On 1st May, Gandhi called this repression as '*Gonda Raj*'. Consequently on 4thMay Gandhi was also arrested. In Harvana also, the Congress Party was declared illegal.[25] Public meetings and demonstrations were prohibited. *Aman Sabhas* were again revived.

In the meanwhile, the British Government decided to proceed with the Round Table Conference, regardless of the Congress attitude. It proved futile. In January 1931 Gandhi was released. The members of the Congress Working Committee also were released on January 26, 1931 and on 5th March, the Gandhi-Irwin Pact was concluded. The Civil Disobedience Movement was suspended and all the prisoners were released.

At the juncture the execution of Bhagat Singh, Raj Guru and Sukh Dev on 23rd March 1931 excited great resentment throughout the country. At Karachi the Congress Session was held on 29th March 1931 in which 17 Congressmen from Haryana participated. Gandhi was allowed to represent the Congress at the Second Round Table Conference. But it also proved unsuccessful. Gandhi resumed the Civil Disobedience Movement. Again the Wholesale arrests were made. Gandhi was arrested in January 1932.

The Government made strenuous-efforts to crush the movement. In Haryana a number of public meetings were held at Karnal and Rohtak districts. Government adopted repressive measures. People were charged with *Lathis* at certain places. Houses were searched. Leaders like Sham Lal Advocate, Shri Ram Sharma and Neki Ram Sharma were arrested. In Ambala 60, Karnal 45, Gurgaon 28, Rohtak 350 and Hissar 73 people were arrested.

The Movement continued, however, it led to frustration and confusion. It was suspended in May 1933 and finally withdrawn in May 1934.

Like most other Gandhi's movements, the Civil Disobedience Movement, apparently failed yet it marked a step forwards towards the national consciousness. Gandhi checked the revolutionary activities in the country but demonstrated the country's resentment against the Government policies. It inculcated the feelings of patriotism, self-reliance and sacrifice among the people and loss of faith and confidence in British Regime.

The Constitutional Development (1930-38)

In the meanwhile in September 1930, the election to the Fourth Reformed Council was held. This time the main parties which participated in the election were the Congress, the Unionist Party and the Hindu Mahasabha. Out of the nine constituencies from Haryana region four seats were won by the Congress, the successful candidates were Mam Raj Singh Chauhan (Ambala), Nathu Singh (Karnal), Joti Prasad (Hissar) and Sajjan Kumar (Hissar). Balbir Singh (Gurgaon) was elected on Hindu Mahasabha ticket and four seats were secured by the Unionist Party. The winners were Allaha Dad Khan (Ambala), Yasin Khan (Gurgaon), Chhotu Ram (Rohtak) and Ram Swarup (Hissar). During Oct./ Nov. 1934, the election for the Central Legislative Assembly was held and Sham Lal of Congress Party was elected to the Assembly from Ambala Division.[27] During the period, the Unionist Party played a significant role. Sir Fazl-i-Husain was called to form a ministry. He took Sir Chhotu Ram in his Council of Ministers. The period followed a lull of political activity after the failure of the Civil Disobedience Movement in 1934.

In 1937 the election fever again gave some impetus to the political activity. According to the Act of 1935, the number of the elected members of Punjab Legislative Council had been increased. Now in the House of 175 members, the membership from Haryana was raised from nine to twenty-two. Now the Congress, the Nationalist Party, the Unionist Party and the Hindu Mahasabha were the main contestants.

Great efforts were made by the Congress to win the election. The Congress contested all the 22 seats. Shri Ram Sharma and Hardev Sahai were incharge of the Congress campaign in Haryana. Similarly Sir Chhotu Ram and Rao Balbir Singh were the main propagators for the Unionist Party and the Hindu Mahasabha respectively. Mrs. Sarojini Naidu and Jawaharlal Nehru made extensive tour of Haryana and addressed many public meetings. Swami Satya Dev, a prominent Arya Samaj leader, also made marked impression through his eloquent speeches at Ambala and Jagadhri. Similarly, Sir Fazl-i-Husain and Sir Chhotu Ram toured for the Unionist success. Raja Narendra Nath visited various places for the Hindu Mahasabha candidates. Pandit Madan Mohan Malaviya toured for the Nationalist Party.

In this eventful election, the twenty-two seats from Haryana were filled as foliows:

Name of the Party	*No. of candidates won*
Unionist	12
Congress	4
Hindu Mahasabha	1
Independents	5
	Total 22

This was the first time that the Unionist Party got more than 50% seats. The Congress lost its position. In Punjab, Sir Sikander Hayat Khan, the Unionist Leader, was called to form ministry. He formed his six men cabinet 3 Muslims, 2 Hindus and 1 Sikh. From Haryana Chaudhry Chhotu Ram and Chaudhry Tikka Ram were selected.

Next two years witnessed the clash between the Congress and the Unionist Party. The Congress tried to strengthen its base among the peasants in Haryana. Keeping this in view a Punjab Provincial Conference was held at Rohtak in March 1938.[28] It was attended by Bhulabhai Desai, Lahri Singh, Gopi Chand Bhargava, Joginder Singh and Raizada Hansraj.[29] On the other hand Sir Chhotu Ram and Sir Sikander Hayat Khan, the Unionist leaders, toured Panipat, Rohtak, Rewari, Hissar and addressed public meetings.[30]

Soon it led to the rivalry between the Congress and the Unionist Party. In a meeting some Congressmen were beaten by the Unionist workers. As a protest a Haryana Political Conference was also held at Rohtak in October, 1938.[31] It condemned the assault on Congress workers by the Unionist Party.

The Famine in Haryana 1938-1939

Besides the clash between the Congress and the Unionist workers, the end of the year 1938 witnessed a severe famine due to complete failure of rains in Hissar and in the parts of Gurgaon and Rohtak districts.[32]

A large number of human beings and the cattle died of starvation. Many people took to dacoity and robbery.[33] It is estimated that about a lakh of people became homeless. Nearly four out of six lakh of cattle were either sold or perished.[34]

The Congress made sincere efforts to help the famine striken people.[35] *A Congress Qahat Committee* (Congress Famine Relief Committee) was formed in September 1938.[36] Neki Ram Sharma, Thakur Das Bhargava and Hardev Sahai were its President, Vice-President and Secretary respectively. They visited the affected areas and met Sir Sikander Hayat Khan and Sir Chhotu Ram to modify the Famine Code.[37] S.C. Bose, the President of the All-India Congress, also visited Hissar, Bhiwani and Rohtak in November 1939.[38] Later, Swami Brahmanand, the Congress leader, toured the affected areas and went on Hunger strike at Hissar on the issue in Dec. 1939.[39] Gandhi also made appeal through the Press for help. The above committee rendered a lot to help the victims in 1938-39.[40]

To solve the famine problem on a sound footing, the immediate implementation of the Bhakra Dam Project was demanded. In a Conference at Hissar on May 19, 1939, the Government was vehementally criticised for its step-motherly treatment to the people of Haryana.[41] Neki Ram Sharma called the project as a 'question of life and death[42] for the people and warned that if the demand of a canal was not fulfilled by 29th Feb. 1940, there would be a mass movement."[43] Some nominal relief operations like 'Work Camps', Gratuitous Relief', 'Spinning Centres' etc. were also carried out by the Government.[44] But the famine wages were very low. In fact they were attached with the price of wheat as shown in the table on page 135.[45]

People of Haryana were badly distressed by the famine, but soon the world War II was declared, so no attention was paid to their difficulties.

Date *(Examp-les only*	*Price of wheat (per Rupee) Seer*	*Wages in pie per day* *Special (e.g. mates, cooksy etc.*	*Diggers (Heavy Workers)*	*Carriers light workers*	*Children 10-16*
August, 1939	14	6	5	4	3
December, 1939	9	9	8	6	4
June. 1940	12	7	5	5	3

The Hyderabad Satyagraha: (30th Jan. 1939 to 17th August 1939)

Before we turn towards the Second World War and the subsequent happenings, two significant events cannot be ignored. These were the Hyderabad Satyagraha and the Loharu incident, in which the people of Haryana participated enthusiastically. Though the Hyderabad State was ruied by a Muslim called 'Nizam', its main population was Hindu. According to the census of 1936 the Hindus constituted 87% of the population and the Muslims only 10%. The Muslim community could not tolerate the dominating Hindu position. Many of the state officers dreamt of a Muslim State. In 1937 out of total 1,331 state officers, only 316 were Hindus,[47] Certain restrictions were imposed on the right of worship. Some fanatic Muslim officers planned to curb the Arya Samaj activities in the State. Consequently, the Arya Samaj was declared illegal, and anti-government. The Arya Samajists were deprived of all types of religious facilities. They were shadowed by the C.I.D. They were debarred from preaching their doctrine, constructing their temples and organising their Samaj.

The Arya Samaj made tremendous efforts for six years[48] to amicably solve the problem. But in vain. Consequently, the Arya Samaj planned a *Satyagraha* under the leadership of Mahatma Narayana Swami[49] and Swami Swantranand. A Satyagraha Samiti was formed in October 1938. At Sholapur, an all India Arya Samaj Conference was held which was presided over by Anne on January 22, 1939. The 'Hyderabad Day' was celebrated.[50] On 30th January, 1939 the Satyagraha Samiti declared *Satyagraha*. The chief dictators of the various groups of the *Satyagrahis* were Mahatma Narayan Swami, Kauver Chand Kiran Sharda of Rajasthan, Mahatma Khushal Chand Khursand of Punjab, Dhurendra Shastri, Pandit Vedvarth, Mahashya Krishan of Punjab, Pandit Gyanendra of Gujarat and Vinayak Rao of Hyderabad.[51]

In this agitation, the people of Haryana took leading part,[52] under the leadership of Swami Swantranand, Mahatma Khushal Chand and Mahashya Krishan. The Satyagraha Samitis were formed in all the important towns and villages. At several places more than five *jathas* were sent. For example, the Satyagraha Samiti of Rohtak District sent four *Jathas* from *Gurukul* Bhanswal under the leadership of Acharya Harish Chandra, Swami Brahmanand, Choudhry Newnand Singh, and Satya Priya respectively. Bhagat Phul Singh was one of the moving forces in this agitation.

Similarly other *Jathas* were sent from the *Gurukuls* of Gharunda, Matindu, Jhajjar, Kurukshetra and Gundpuri. In Hissar District Pandit Murari Lal and Mansha Ram prepared the ground. In Sirsa Ganganand and Nityanand made tremendous efforts. From Jind seven *Jathas* were sent. Perhaps, there was no significant town of Haryana, where the people did not participate.

The Hyderabad Government adopted all the repressive measures. The *Satyagrahis* were beaten mercilessly. Bad food was provided. No medical aid was given in the jails.

It is estimated that up to 8th August 1939 nearly 10,579 people were in jails.[53] Nearly 28 *Satyagrahis* died in the Jails. Sunehere Singh of Butana (Distt. Rohtak) and Fakir Chand of Sherda (Distt. Kurukshetra) died in the jail due to the absence of medical help.[54] Similarly, Matu Ram of Miland (Distt. Hissar) and Rati Ram of Sampla (Distt. Rohtak) also died in the jails.[55]

Anyhow, the Hyderabad State was compelled to change its decision and gave the right of worship on 19th July 1939 to all the Arya Samajs. And finally on 17th August 1939, the *Satyagrah* was withdrawn.

Perhaps it was one of the most successful agitations. While it gave impetus and confidence to the national awakening in Hyderabad State, it equally roused a feelings of self-sacrifice, discipline and confidence among the people of Haryana. Though a religious movement it aroused their national feelings. Now the people of Haryana, especially the Arya Samajists began to look for the religious atrocities in their own region. The Loharu state provided them an opportunity.

The Loharu Incident: (29th March, 1941)

The success of Hyderabad Satyagrah had a deep impact on the people of Haryana. In fact, it boosted up the moral of the *Satyagrahis*. Now they were in a mood to fight against the religions atrocities in their own region.

In Haryana region, there were only some small states which inclnded Pataudi, Dujana, Jind and partly Patiala and Nabha. People of these states were dissatisfied because of the repressive attitude and coercive policies of their rulers. Heavy taxation, the system of *Begar*, and the religious restrictions were generally the causes of discontents. Efforts were already made by Praja Mandal Party to get some of these grievances redressed.

Like Hyderabad, the ruler of Loharu was a Muslim, while its population was predominently Hindu. According to 1941 Census its total population was 27,892. Hindus constituted nearly 95%. The ruler of this state also obstructed the activties of Arya Samaj which was established in April 1940. Pandit Ganganath Satyarthi and Thakur Bhagat Singh were its local leaders.[56] In May-July 1940 certain Arya Samajists preachers like Hardayal, Salig Ram and Mansa Ram went there.[57] Finally the local Arya Samaj decided to celebrate its annual function on 29th March, 1941. Proper arrangements were made. Permission had been sought.[58] Unfortunately, the procession was stopped and attacked near a mosque. Consequently, more than sixty persons were wounded.[59]

This event created a feeling of revenge and antagonism. Some articles highlighting the incident were written. Representations were made to the Political Agent. In fact, this incident kindled a ray of hope among the depressed people and they started movements in their respective states.

The Quit India Movement

In September 1939 the Second World War broke out. Lord Linlithgow, the Viceory of India, also declared war and sent Indian troops abroad. While in the first world war, all the people helped the Government by men, money and material but this time the public opinion was different. The Congress party refused to cooperate with the Government of India on account of dragging India into War without Consulting her.[60] The Congress withdrew its members from the Central Legislature and all the Congress provincial Ministers resigned. Perhaps this was the beginning of non-cooperation which ended in the Quit India Movement.[61] Only big *Zamidars*, princes and the Unionist Party helped the Government. The Muslims remained neutral.

The Congress appealed to the people to refrain from recruitment as well as donations. Rather it pressed the Government to accept the genuine demands of the country. Again the Congress Committees were reorganised throughout the country and conferences were held.

In Haryana a Rural Conference was held at Village Jasawarkhari (10 miles from Hissar) in which the role of the loyalists was vehementally criticised. The Government tried to disrupt the proceedings, but failed. In Karnal District at Kheri Village another Conference was held under the leadership of Lala Duni Chand.

The August 1940 offer could not meet the demands. In fact the Congress reaction was reflected in the shape of Individual *Satyagrah*. Gandhi gave call for an individual *Satyagrah* on 17th October 1940. He declared that one individual at a time should go out in the Street shouting anti-war slogan and should get himself arrested. In fact only selected individuals offered themselves for arrest. Nearly 23,223 people were arrested.[62]

In Haryana also, some of the Congress leaders offered themselves for the *Satyagrah*. Pt. Neki Ram Sharma was the first *Satyagrahi* of Haryana who offered himself on 5th December, 1940 at Bhiwani.[63] Nearly more than six hundred people were arrested in Haryana.[64]

The individual *Satyagrah* cut no ice. After a couple of months, when Cripps Mission failed, the Congress Working Committee passed the Quit India resolution at Wardha on 14th July, 1942. The All India Congress Committee met again at Bombay on 7th August 1942 to consider the Resolution.

In fact, it was the last political movement under the leadership of Mahatma Gandhi. During this movement generally the upper class-rich people, landlords and princes helped the Government. Muslims generally remained aloof. The labour under the influence of the Communist Party or Radical Party did not participate while the labour under the influence of the Congress supported the movement[65] Of course, it was the lower middle classes and the peasants who whole-heartedly supported the movement[66]. Perhaps it was student-peasant middle class rebellion.[67] Gandhi gave a call to do or die.[68] The next day, Gandhi and all the prominent leaders of the Congress were arrested. Throughout the country a large number of arrests were made. The Government declared the All India Congress Committee as unlawful association.

The news of the arrests of leaders spread like a wildfire. *Hartals* and public meetings were organised. The movement soon took a violent shape. The Government of India took it very seriously. In a letter to the Prime Minister Churchill, Lord Linlithgow, called it as 'most serions rebellion sinee that of 1857'.[69]

In Haryana, it gathered some momentum. In fact it liad no appreciable strength in this region.[70] The Muslims and Sikhs having strong traditions of military services remained mainly uninvolved.[71] All the Congress Committees were declared unlawful on 10th August 1942. Local leaders were arrested.

Even the family members of the arrested were shadowed and harassed by the C.I.D. men. In Sonepat *tehsil* the police adopted very coercive methods[72]. In Gurgaon the demonstrations were subjected to indiscriminate *lathi*-charges.[73] Babu Hari Harlal, a labour leader, was arrested and beaten ruthlessly for having obstructed the construction of an aerodrome near Gurgaon.[74] In Ambala the office of the District Congress Committee was sealed and the property was confiscated.[75] However, typed copies of the Quit India Resolution were distributed. Neki Ram Sharma who attended the Bombay meeting was arrested on 14th August 1942 at Bhiwani.[76] During August 1942 to May 1944 *i.e.* till the suspension of the movement, the following arrests were made:[77]

Year	*Ambala*	*Karnal*	*Gurgaon*	*Rohtak*	*Hissar*
1942	114	72	115	239	151
1943	124	377	535	402	333
1944	60	299	158	150	51

Like other places in Haryana also, nearly 4 Railway Stations were attacked, 11 post offices burnt, at 45 places Telegraph Wires cut, 8 Government buildings including Police Stations attacked and 6 Railway lines were eut.[78]

However the Quit India Movement also failed. In Haryana it had a little impact on the political life of the people. As Haryana was under a strong Unionist Ministry and the student community was not so strong it could not prove effective in the region.

The Indian National Army

Though the people of Haryana did not take much part in the war, but they played a notable role by enlisting themselves as members of the Indian National Army in 1942. Its main object was to wage war against the British. They believed in organised revolt. As early as in 1938 Subhash Bose appealed for more effective methods than what Mahatma Gandhi had produced.[79] Soon the INA was formed with the battle cry "Delhi Chalo."

As regards Haryana, as many as 2248 soldiers[80] joined the Indian National Army. The highest number of soldiers was from Gurgaon District *i.e.* 986 and the next was from Rohtak District *i.e.* 873. Out of these participants nearly 273 gave their lives for India's freedom.[81]

About 17,000 men of Indian National Army were brought back to India as prisoners of war. They were tried in Red Fort, Delhi for waging war against the King. The Congress Party also appointed a Defence Committee for their release. It included Bhulabhai Desai, Tej Bahadur Sapru and Jawaharlal Nehru. The trial proceedings aroused public interest.[82] Jawaharlal Nehru along with Neki Ram Sharma visited Haryana in 1946, and gave call to a Relief Fund for the defence of the Indian National Army's prisoners and to support their dependents.[83]

Although the Indian National Army could not succeed in its own way, but its impact cannot be ignored. It gave a new life to the freedom movement and helped to bring the goal nearer. The Indian National Army showed unique example of communal harmony and comradeship.[84] In fact it was a warning to the British that they could no longer rely upon the loyalty of the Indian mercenary troops.[85] It proved that Indian soldiers were not mere mercenary but more patriotic.[86]

Post War Developments 1945-47

After the termination of the Second World War, the elections of the Central and Provincial Legislatures were held in December, 1945. Now the main contestants were the Congress party, the Unionist and the Muslim League. In fact, the elections were held in a profoundly agitated mood.[87]

In Punjab, the Unionist Party was not so popular now. It was partly due to the death of its prominent leaders like Sh. Fazl-i-Husain, Sir Chhotu Ram and Sir Sikander Hayat Khan, and partly due to the changing attitude of the Government. Earlier the British supported Sir Sikander Hayat Khan now it was inclined towards Jinnah *i.e.* the Muslim League. In this election the Muslim league secured the highest seats.

The party position of various groups was as follows:

Name of the Party/Group	*Elected from Punjab Region*	*Elected from Haryana Region*	*Total*
Congress	40	11	51
Muslim League	69	6	75
Akali	22	–	22
Unionist	16	4	20
Independent	7	–	7
Total	154	21	175

The above table clearly indicates that while Muslim League got highest seats in Punjab region, the Congress won the highest seats in Haryana. In spite of its being the largest group, the Muslim League could not form Ministry. On the other hand, all the other four groups combined together and formed a coalition government under Khizar Hyat Khan. This enranged the Muslim League and they started a campaign against the coalition government. Consequently, Khizar Hyat Khan resigned in March 1946 and the Punjab passed under the Governor's rule.[88]

In March a series of communal riots again started. These riots took place in some parts of North-Western Punjab. According to an estimate the casualties ran in thousands.[89] In Haryana also communal riots started at Rohtak, Hissar and Gurgaon.[90] Migration too had started though on a small scale. In April, May and June the Meos in Gurgaon became the victims of the revenge.[91] A number of villages were burnt, houses were plundered, people were slaughtered and property was looted. Troops were called to control the situation.[92] The Gurgaon District was declared a dangerously disturbed area.[93] On 1st August the Boundary Commission was set up. The communal passion led to country's division and on 15th August, 1947 India and Pakistan were declared as separate independent countries.

NOTES

1. Manoranjan Jha: *Civil Disobedience Movement and After*, (Meerut, 1973), p. 68.
2. D.G. Tendulkar; *op. cit.*, Vol. II, p. 24.
3. *Ibid.*
4. S.C. Bose: *The Indian Struggle*, 1920-42, (Bombay, 1964), p. 82.
5. *The Tribune*, 8-8-1930.
6. *Ibid.*, 23-4-1930.
7. *Ibid.*
8. *Home Dept.* (*Political*), *Govt. of India, Jan. 1930, File 250.*
9. *The Tribune*, 26-4-1930.
10. *Home Dept.* (*Political*), *Govt. of India, Jan. 1930, File 18.*
11. *The Tribune*, 29-4-1930.
12. *Ibid.*, 18-1-1930.
13. *Ibid.*, 13-4-1930.
14. *Ibid.*
15. *Ibid.*, 19-7-1930.
16. *Home Dept.* (*Political*), *Govt. of India, File 170/1920.*
17. *The Tribune*, 3-5-1930.
18. *Ibid.*, 12-8-1930.

19. *Home Dept. (Political), Govt. of India, Sept. 1930, File 18.*
20. *Ibid.*
21. *M.M. Juneja, op. cit.*, p. 86.
22. H.D. Sulug, *op. cit.*, pp. 52-57, *The Tribune*, 12-4-1929.
23. D.G. Tendulkar, *op. cit.*, Vol. II, p. 35.
24. *Ibid.*, p. 36.
25. *The Tribune*, 11-9-1931.
26. *Ibid.*
21. *Ibid.*, 17-11-1934.
28. *Ibid.*, 27-3-1938.
29. *Ibid.*, 29-3-1938.
30. *Ibid.*, 11-10-1938.
31. *Ibid.*, 9-10-1938.
32. En Mangat Rai: *Commitment My Style, Carreer in the Indian Civil Service*, (Vikas, Delhi, 1973), p. 66.
33. *Neki Ram Sharma's Papers.*
34. *A.I.C.C. File, p. 17,1939-40.*
35. *The Tribune*, 19-10-1938.
36. *A.I.C.C. File, 1939-40, p. 17.*
37. *Neki Ram Sharma Papers.*
38. *The Tribune*, 30-11-1938.
39. *A.I.C.C. File, 1939-40*, p. 17.
40. *Ibid.*
41. H.D. Sulag, *op. cit.*, p. 66.
42. *Neki Ram Sharma's Papers.*
43. H.D. Sulag, *op. cit.*,p. 66; *See also Lala Sham Lal Papers*; Sadhu Ram Joshi; *Insanyet ke Pehredar*, p. 100.
44. En Mangat Rai,: *op. cit.*, pp. 69-71.
45. *Ibid.*, p. 75.
46. Ramchandra Jayed: *op. cit.*, p. 64; Ranjit Singh; *op. cit.*, p. 49.
47. Ramchandra Jayed: *op. cit.*, p. 64; Dr. Ranjit Singh: *op. cit.*, p. 49.
48. *Balidan Javanti Samriti Granth*, p. 27.
49. *Ibid.*, p. 27.
50. Shri Ramchandra Jayed: *op. cit.*, p. 65.
51. *Ibid.*, p. 66.
52: For detail *see* Dr. Ranjit Singh: *op. cit.*, pp. 49-57; Ramchandra Jayed: *op. cit.*, pp. 64-68.
53. *Balidan Jayanti Samriti Granth*, p. 28.
54. *Ibid.*, p. 114.
55. *Ibid.*, p. 118.
56. Ranjit Singh: *op. cit.*, p. 57.
57. *Ibid.*, p. 58.
58. *Ibid.*
59. *Ibid.*, p. 59.

60. Amba Prasad: *The Revolt of 1942*, p. 9.
61. *Ibid.*
62. *Ibid.*, p. 18,
63. M.M. Juneja: *op. cit.*, p. 48.
64. Jagdish Chander: *op. cit.*, p. 160.
65. Amba Prasad: *op. cit.*, p. 74.
66. *Ibid.*, p. 76.
67. *Ibid.*, p. 77.
68. D.G. Tendulkar: *op. cit.*, Vol. VI, pp. 190-200.
69. P.N. Chopra (Ed.): *Quit India Movement, British Secret Report*, p. 1.
70. Francis G. Hutchines: *Spontaneous Revolution; The Quit India Movement*, (Delhi, Manohar, 1971), p. 286.
71. *Ibid.*
72. A. Moin Zaidi: *The Way Out to Freedom: An Inquiry into the Quit India Movement conducted by Participants*, (Orientalia, New Delhi, 1973), p. 91.
73. *Ibid.*
74. *Ibid.*
75. *Ibid.*, p. 92.
76. *The Tribune*, 16-8-1942.
77. *Jagdish Chander*: *op. cit.*, p. 163.
78. *Ibid.*, p. 164.
79. S.C. Bose: *op. cit.*, p. 337.
80. Jagdish Chander: *op. cit.*, p. 163.
81. *Ibid.*, p. 164.
82. Tara Chand; *History of the Freedom Movement in India*, Vol. IV, (Delhi, Public Div., 1972), p. 458.
83. S. Gopal: *Jawaharlal Nehru's Biography*, Vol. I. (Dec. 1976), p. 308.
84. Tara Chand; *op. cit.*, p. 423.
85. *Ibid.*
86. *Ibid.*
87. *Ibid.*, p. 561.
88. *Ibid.*, p. 562.
89. *Ibid.*, p. 563.
90. *Ibid.*, The Tribune, 15-3-1947.
91. Tara Chand: *op. cit.*, p. 563.
92. *The Tribune*, 15-3-1947.
93. *Ibid.*, 25-3-1947.

8

Formation of the State (1947-1966)

The declaration of the independence of India was received with mixed feelings. It had led to the unprecedented exchange of a considerable portion of the population. Besides this, it also resulted into a wild erruption of passions on both sides of the newly fixed border and there were widespread communal riots. These riots were termed as 'civil war' by Stephen[1] and as the 'war of succession' by Breacher.[2] The region of Haryana also witnessed a series of communal riots, particularly in the districts[3] of Karnal, Gurgaon, and Rohtak. The feeling of revenge and of retalialion reigned supream and the love of plunder added fuel to the fire. These riots created a feeling of insecurity and fear.

There was a considerable Muslim population in the region of Haryana as indicated by the table given below:[4]

Districts	*Percentage of Muslims*	*Percentage of Sikhs*	*Percentage of (Others Approx.)*
Hissar	28.2	6.0	64.8
Rohtak	17.2	0.1	81.7
Gurgaon	33.5	–	66.8.
Karnal	30.6	2.0	67.0
Ambala	31.6	18.4	48.7

As the above table indicates, the maximum number of the Muslim population was in the Gurgaon District. About 1,25,000 Meos from this district shifted to the refugee camps. But they were evacuated in a limited number. The Government of India, due to the fear of the world opinion, decided to keep them in

India. In addition to the Meos of Gurgaon District, a proposal was put forward and accepted to settle about 15,000 Meos belonging to the States of Alwar and Bharatpur recently displaced in the riots. The area of Nuh and Ferozepur-Jhirka tehsils was declared non-refugee area.[5] Nearly 10,000 Hindus and Sikhs refugees who were allotted land in this area were asked to vacate it.[6]

Migration and Rehabilitation

Nearly 50 lakhs, Hindus including Sikhs from West Pakistan left for India during August-September 1947. Within a week after the 15th August 1947 nearly 11 lakhs refugees had arrived in East Punjab and in the following weeks another 25 lakhs were received.[7] The evacuation work was done by trains, road transport and on foot. Nearly 673 trains evacuated 27,94,368 refugees from August 1947 to November 1947.[8] Similarly about 12 lakhs came through road transport,[9] and nearly 8,49,000 reached East Punjab for shelter and security on foot.[10] They brought with them the sad tales of atrocities, murder, looting, arson and blood shedding.

Great efforts were made by the Government and the private agencies to rehabilitate the people from the West Pakistan. It was decided to have one big Refugee Camp at Kurukshetra of capacity up to five lakhs, and several other camps at Amritsar, Gurdaspur, Jullundur, Ludhiana and Ambala.[11] In Middle of November 1947 the Kurukshetra Camp had 1,75,000 refugees.[12] The people were also sent to Ambala, Hissar, Gurgaon and Karnal. By the end of November the total camp population in Haryana had shot up to 7,20,000,[13] out of which Kurukshetra camp had 2,75,000.

After sometime, the government decided to construct 4,000 houses in 12 towns at an estimated cost of ₹ 2.50 crores.[14] It included several towns of Haryana namely Jagadhri, Karnal, Panipat, Sonepat, Gurgaon, Rewari and Palwal.[15] Then proposal was also made to build 200 houses at Hissar and another 200 houses at Ambala.[16] Hansi, Sirsa, Bhiwani, Bahadurgarh, Samalkha were considered for the sub-urban development.[17] Three new townships were considered for the accommodation of 1,20,000 of refugees.[18] Sites selected for the purpose were Faridabad, Ballabhgarh and Sonepat.

As regards tbe voluntary organizations, the Shiromani Gurudwara Prabandhak Committee and the Rashtriya Swayam-sewak Sangh made considerable efforts for rehabilitation of a large part of the refugees in the East Punjab.[19]

The approximate number of refugees accommodated in Haryana region is given district-wise as follows:[20]

District	*Refugees accommodated*
Ambala	1,94,403
Karnal	3,25,173
Rohtak	1,41,695
Hissar	1,55,959
Gurgaon	60,794

Keeping in view the above table, it can be summarised that the region of Haryana accommodated a good number of refugees. Whereas the people who left Haryana were mostly artisans, the bulk of the new immigrants consisted of the Jat Sikhs of the formerly canal colonies and the Hindus and Sikhs belonging to business and professional classes. While concentration of the Sikhs took place in the western part of the East Punjab, the bulk of non-Sikhs settled in the Haryana region.

These immigrants considerably affected the prevailing conditions. They had brought with them a different way of life. The struggle for survival further aggravated the situation. In fact, they were not satisfied with their present lot, Their presence encouraged the emergence of new social groups, conflicts and tensions. The resentment was soon reflected in the shape of the language and religious conflicts. The language problem soon became a bone of contention and centre of all political activity. The refugees soon became an significant factor in the future political considerations of the State,[21] and eventually gave impetus to the demand of statehood for Haryana.

Origin of the Demand for a Separate State

However, it would be wrong to say that the demand of Haryana was made due to the fear of penetration of Punjab displaced persons is every walk of the life the region.[22] Similarly it is also incorrect to say that it was a part of the post partition development,[23] or it was off spring of the demand for the Punjabi Suba.

The origin of the demand of the Haryana State can be visualised in its historical perspective. The seeds of dissatisfaction can be seen among the Haryanvis due to the step-motherly treatment given by the British from 1858 onwards and the Punjab Government during the 1950's. As we have studies earlier, the Haryana region was tagged with the Punjab in 1858 as a 'political punishment' to the people of this region. Of course, it was only their political isolation but they were still more related socially and culturally to the people of Delhi and the western U.P. They had lost the political boundaries but they maintained the cultural ties of *Roti* and *Beti*.

Perhaps it was due to the continued repressive policy of the British Govt. that no significant development was made in the region in the sphere of the education, trade, industry, means of communications and irrigation. Consequently, it remained backward socially, educationally, economically and politically throughout the 19th century.

With the transfer of the Capital to Delhi, the Haryana region was further isolated. In 1920's certain changes in Delhi State were suggested. The Muslim League also suggested the extension of the boundaries of Delhi with the inclusion of Agra, Meerut and Ambala Division in it.[24] In 1928, All Parties Conference at Delhi again made demand for the extension of the boundaries of Delhi.[25] A similar demand was made to Sir J.P. Thompson, the Commissioner of Delhi by the people.[26] Some of the prominent Haryana leaders Mke Pandit Neki Ram Sharma, Lala Deshbandhu Gupta and Shri Ram Sharma met Gandhi and requested him that the districts of Haryana region be merged with Delhi.[27] In 1931 at the second Round Table Conference, Sir Geoffrey Corbert, Financial Commissioner of the Punjab Government and Secretary of the Indian Delegation to the Round Table Conference, suggested the reorganisation of the Punjab boundaries and the separation of the Ambala Division from the Punjab.[28] He argued, 'historically Ambala Division is a part of Hindustan and its inclusion in the province of the Punjab was an incident of British rule. Its language is Hindustani, not Punjabi and its people are akin to the people of adjoining Meerut and Agra Divisions.'[29]

In 1932, Lata Deshbandu Gupta of Panipat forcefully stated that, 'Hindi speaking region had never been a part of Punjab. Even since its inclusion in Punjab, the region had been suffering economically, politically and culturally. It was essential for the development of the region to separate it from Punjab proper and form a new state by uniting with it certain adjoining parts of Delhi, Rajasthan and of the U.P.'[30]

In fact, the demand of the creation of the 'Greater Delhi' or 'Vishal Haryana' was actively supported by several leaders like Mahatma Gandhi, Motilal-Nehru, Asaf Ali, Sir Chhotu Ram and Pandit Thakur Das Bhargava.[31]

Formation of the Haryana State

Along with the demand for the Greater Delhi or Vishal Haryana the idea for a Sikh State sprang up as early as 1942.[32] But with the migration of the Muslims from the East Punjab, in 1947, the problem of language was eliminated for the time being. However, the Sachar-Giani formula of October 1, 1949 could not satisfy the Hindus or the Sikhs. According to it the State was divided into two linguistic regions—Punjabi and Hindi. It was decided that the language of the region was to be the medium of instruction in all the schools up to the matriculation stage.

The formula was vehementally criticised. It was called as the 'child of the Giani Kartar Singh'.[33] Protest meetings were held and the signature campaign started. In fact, the language issue soon took the shape of communal strife and antagonism among the Hindus and the Sikhs.

The community-wise position in 1951 in the Hindi speaking region was as shown on Page 150.[34]

The table on next page indicates that the Sikhs were in considerable number in Ambala and Simla districts, while the Muslims had their say in Gurgaon District. So except Ambala

District	*Percentage of Hindus*	*Percentage of Sikhs*	*Percentage of other communities*
Simla	80.8	16.1	3.1
Kangra	97.0	2.0	1.0
Hissar	91.3	7.7	1.0
Rohtak	98.5	0.7	0.8
Gurgaon	82.0	0.7	17.3
Karnal	90.3	8.9	0.8
Ambala	72.2	24.6	3.3
Mahendergarh	98.9	0.6	0.5
	88.8	9.0	2.2
Total	89.5	6.9	3.6

District, the Sikhs population was at the most 9% in other districts. Besides the language issue, the Hindu leaders of the Haryana region opposed the formula on other grounds. They saw undue domination of the Punjabi speaking area in accepting the formula. They felt that it would harm the general interest of the Hindu community.

In the Punjabi speaking region also it acquired a new magnitude. It divided the people on the religious ground. Similarly, the formation of Andhra and the Congress Plan of formation of linguistic state intensified this language conflict in Punjab.[35] Consequently the demand for a Punjabi Speaking Province was made. The first general election in Punjab was fought in 1952 on this issue. But the Akalis who represented the demand got only 13 seats. Perhaps the demand was not popular and it was called as 'fanatic, outmoded, against the spirit of the Age and the creation of a few unbalanced persons.'[36] It was termed as 'a project of the separate tendencies.'[37] It was criticised as 'dangerous to the integrity safety, progress and prosperity.'[38] The demand was called as 'communal or a Sikh state under the clock of language.'[39] The demand was vehementally criticised by the Hindu Mahasabha, Bhartiya Jan Sangh and All Party Maha Punjab Front Samiti. They demanded the creation of a greater Punjab and criticised the Akali's demand as 'merely a whitewash for the attainment of the Sikh hegemony and establishment of this as a base for the future sovereign Sikh state.'[40]

Contrary to the above, the Akali Dal vigorously campaigned for the demand and saw it the 'only way to pursue the language, culture and religion of the Sikhs.' They demanded the merger of the Punjabi speaking area of Punjab, Pepsu and Rajasthan.[41]

The Government of India appointed an All India State Reorganisation Commission on 29th October 1953 to view the reorganisation of the Indian Provinces. Its members were Justice Fazal Ali, Sri Kavelem Madhave Panikkar and Hirdey Nath Kunjru. The Delhi Vidhan Sabha passed a resolution recommending the creation of Maha Delhi or Vishal Haryana.[42] The Commission considered the question of reorganisation and recommended the merger of the PEPSU area into Punjab region and the districts of Mahendergarh and Jind into Haryana region.

However, the Commission rejected the demand of greater Delhi or Vishal Haryana on the ground that 'the separation of

Haryana areas of Punjab which are deficient areas will be no remedy for any ills, real or imaginery, from which this area at present suffers.'[43] Similarly the State Reorganisation Commission rejected the demand of creation of a separate Punjabi Suba. Its main arguments[44] were the lack of popular support, difficulty of demarcating linguistic boundaries, opposition of a large section of the Punjab population, no real language problem and that the demand would not solve the problem of internal tensions.

The Arya Samaj played a dynamic role in the struggle. It demanded that the question of medium of instruction in the educational institutions should be left entirely to the parents. A Hindi Raksha Samiti was also formed and it called for agitation. In 1957 a number of deputations met the then Chief Minister of Punjab and the Prime Minister of India. But all the efforts proved futile. Perhaps, neither the Government of India was in a position to take the decision nor the Government of Punjab was in a situation to suggest the way out due to the peculiar situation of the Congress Party in Punjab.

During the Satyagraha some untowered incidents took place. For example, at Bahu Akbarpur (7 miles from Rohtak), people who wanted to provide food to the Satyagrahis were beaten by the police.[45] Later Pandit Mauli Chand Sharma and Algu Rai Shastri visited this place.

However, the Hindi Raksha Samiti was compelled to call off the Satyagraha in December 1957. It failed due to the lack of popular support and the harsh attitude of the Punjab Government. In fact it remained, more or less, a Hindu-educated middle class movement and could not get momentum among the rural masses. Its also failed due to the want of popular leadership and the alienation of persons like Shri Suraj Bhan, latter the Vice-Chancellor of the Punjab University, Chandigarh.

The Good Relation Committee was established on August 1, 1958.[45] But the Government could not settle the issue. In fact the suggestion of the movement gave handle to Master Tara Singh and his followers. Now the Akali Dal started vigorous movement for the Punjabi Suba.

Meanwhile the Government of India made another attempt to prevent the division of Punjab. A new system known as Regional Formula was introduced. It was to accept the respective claims of the Hindi and Punjabi language without the division of the

State. In the formula both the languages were given the status of the official language up to the district level. Consequently the separate regional committees were set up.

However, this system did not succeed in the coming five years 1960-1965. Demand of the Punjabi speaking Province became more pressing. Nearly 40,000 people including Master Tara Singh were arrested.[46] Even the Prime Minister of India, criticised the Punjabi Suba Agitation and called it a 'tamasha' in his Red Fort speech of 15th August 1960. In 1961 he again said that the Punjabi Suba is a 'communal demand even though it is given a linguistic base.'[47]

During the communal strife and agitation, the Government of Punjab gazetted the establishment of the Haryana Vikash Committee on 2nd March 1961. It was to give suggestions for the social and economic uplift of the region. Shri Ram Sharma was appointed its Chairman with Chaudhary Chand Ram, Rao Nihal Singh and G.L. Bansal as its members.[48] It sent its recommendations after nine months.

On Sept. 23, 1965 the Government of India appointed a Parliamentary Committee under the Chairmanship of Sardar Hukam Singh, Speaker Lok Sabha, to study the question of the division of Punjab. This Committee submitted its report on March 18, 1966. A number of memoranda were presented by the representatives of Haryana Lok Samiti, Haryana All Parties Action Committee, Haryana Arya Samaj and other organizations.[49] This committee recommended the creation of a Punjabi speaking State and also proposed the establishment of a Hindi Speaking state of Haryana. It also recommended the inclusion of Ghandigarh and Kharar Tehsils in Haryana.

The Government of India accepted most of its recommendations and set up Shah Commission popularly known as 'Punjab Boundary Commission' to settle the boundaries of the new states.[50] The Punjab Reorganization Bill was passed by the Parliament on 10th September 1966 and on November 1,1966 Haryana as the seventeenth state of India came into existence.[51]

NOTES

1. Ian Stephens, *Pakistan*, (London, 1963), p. 80.
2. Michael Breacher: *Nehru, A Political Biography*, (*London, 1959*), pp. 318-79.
3. For details *see* Darbara Singh: *The Punjab Tragedy* (*Amritsar, 1949*), pp. 273-74, and 284.

4. M.S. Randhawa: *Out of the Ashes, An Account of the Rehabilitation of Refugees from West Pakistan in Rural Areas of East Punjab,* (Jullundur, 1954), p. 9.
5. A.N. Bali; *Now it can be Told,* (Jullundur, 1949), p. 112.
6. *Ibid.*
7. M.S. Randhawa: *op. cit.*, p. ix.
8. *Ibid.*, p. 26.
9. *Ibid.*
10. *Ibid.*
11. *Ibid.*, p. 30.
12. *Ibid.*
13. *Ibid.*, p. 30.
14. *One Step Forward: East Punjab Achievement* (1947-48).
15. *Ibid.*
16. *Ibid.*
17. *Ibid.*
18. *Ibid.*
19. A.N. Bali; *op. cit.*, p. 138. The Pakistan Govt. alleged the Sikhs and the R.S.S. to kill the Muslims in a planned manner. It published certain pamphlets like *A Note on the Sikh Plan, Rashtriya Sawayam Sewak Sangh, and Sikh Plan in Action.*
20. M.S. Randhawa: *op. cit.*, p. III (The table is based on his work).
21. Munilal: *Haryana on High Road to Prosperity,* (Vikas, Delhi, 1974), P. 8.
22. Satya M. Rai: *Partition of the Panjab,*: (Delhi, 1965), pp. 234-35.
23. *Ibid.*
24. Bhagwan Dev, *Vir Bhumi Haryana,* (Jhajjar, 1965), p. 102.
25. *Ibid.*, p. 102.
26. *Ibid.*, p. 103.
27. Shri Ram Sharma: *Haryana Ke Itihas,* p. 93.
28. *The Indian Round Table Conference,* Vol. III, (London, 1932) Appendix No. VI, p. 1431.
29. *Ibid.*
30. *The Hindustan Times,* 9-12-1932.
31. Ranbir Singh: Genesis and exposition of the Demand for Vishal Haryana *Kurukshetra University Research Journal,* Vol. II, No. 1 (Dec.-January 1968), pp. 213-16.
32. Gurcharan Singh Talib and Lal Singh Giani: *Idea of the Sikh State,* (Lahore, n.d.); Karanjit Kaur: *Akali Dal's Contribution in the Freedom Movement* 1920-47 (Unpublished Dissertation, Punjabi University, Patiala, 1978), p. 70.
33. Ghanshyam Singh Gupta; *The Case of Arya Samaj and Regional Language Formula in Punjab,* (Delhi) p. 4.
34. Quoted from Bir Singh Anant: *Master Tara Singh and Punjabi Suba,* (Unpublished Dissertation, Punjabi University, Patiala, 1971-72.
35. *Ibid.*, p. 57.
36. Chandravarkar, *Maha Punjab,* (Hoshiarpur, 1954), p. 4.
37. *Ibid.*, p. 8.
38. *Ibid.*, p. 4.

39. *Ibid.*, p. 5.
40. For detail *see* B.R. Nayar: *Minority Politics in the Punjab*, (Princeton 1966), p. 55; Bir Singh Anant: *op. cit.*, p. 62.
41. *The Spokesman*, 7-9-1955, For the background and the various factors of the demand of the Punjabi Speaking Suba see B.R. Nayar: *op. cit.*, pp. 140-56.
42. For detail *see* State Reorganisation Commission Report, (Delhi, 1955).
43. *Ibid.*
44. Ghanshyam Singh Gupta: *op. cit.*, p. 17.
45. Jay Chand Vidyalankar: *The Language and Script Problem of Punjab*, (Jullundur, 1966), p. xiii.
46. Bir Singh Anant: *op. cit.*, p. 85.
47. *Lok Sabha Debates*, Lvii No. 16. August 28, 1961.
48. Shri Ram Sharma: *Haryana Ka Itihas*, p. 146.
49. *Report of the Parliamentary Committee on the Demand of the Punjabi Suba*, (Delhi, 1965), p. 56.
50. For detail *see Report of the Punjab Boundary Commission*, 1966.
51. Rajendra: "How Haryana became a state, thwarted Aspirations and their fulfilment", *Haryana Review*, iv, 1970, pp. 10-; Muni Lal: *op. cit.*, p. 4.

Appendix I

Proclamation to the Cis-Sutlej Chiefs, 1809

It is clearer than the sun and better proved than the existence of yesterday that the marching of a detachment of British troops to this side of the river Sutlege was entirely at the application and earnest entreaty of the several chiefs, and originated solely from friendly considerations in the British Government to preserve them in their possessions and independence. A treaty having been concluded on the 25th of April, 1809 between Mr. Metcalfe on the part of the British Government and Maharaja Ranjeet Singh, agreeable to the orders of the Right Hon'ble the Governor-General in Council, I have the pleasure of publishing for the satisfaction of the chiefs of the country of Malwah and Sirhind, the pleasure and resolutions of the British Government as contained in the seven following articles :

1. The country of the chiefs of Malwah and Sirhind having entered under the British protection, they shall in future be secured from the authority and influence of Maharaja Ranjeet Singh conformably to the terms of the treaty.
2. All the country of the chiefs thus taken under protection shall be exempted from all pecuniary tribute to the British Government.
3. The chiefs shall remain in the full exercise of the same rights and authority in their own possessions which they enjoyed before they were received under the British protection.
4. Should a British force on purposes of general welfare be required to march through the country of the said chiefs, it is necessary and incumbent that every chief shall within his

own possessions assist and furnish to the full of his power such force with supplies of grain and other necessaries, which may be demanded.

5. Should an enemy approach from any quarter for the purpose of conquering this country, friendship and mutual interest require that chiefs join the British army with all their forces and exerting themselves in expelling the enemy act under discipline and proper obedience.
6. All Europeans article brought by merchants from the eastern districts for the use of the army shall be allowed to pass by the *thannadars* and *Savadars* of the several chiefs without molestation and the demand of duty.
7. All horses purchased for the use of the cavalry regiments» whether in the district of Sirhind or elsewhere, the bringers of which being provided with seated *rahdaries* from the Resident at Dehlie or Officer Commanding at Sirhind, shall be allowed to pass through the country of the said chiefs without molestation or the demand of duty.

Glossary

Aman Sabhas	Peace Committees.
Bania	Merchant; trader; trading class of Hindus.
Begar	Forced labour.
Beti	Daughter.
Chabutra	A platform.
Chalisa	The fortieth.
Charkha	A Spinning-wheel.
Chaudharies	Village headmen. The cultivators who, either on their own account, or as the representative of other members of the village, pays the Government dues and are registered in the collectors roll; minor local chiefs; traditional leaders of a community.
Chowki	A Police post; A garrison; A sub-headquarter.
Daroga-e-shikar	Incharge of the hunting expeditions.
Dharma	Religious Ordinances; rules of conduct.
Durbar	Court; hall of audience.
Dussehra	Autumn festival commemorating Rama's defeat of Ravana.
Faujdar	District Police Chief; (in Marathi) district Military Chief.
Gunda Raj	A Rogue government.
Goshala	A shelter for cows.
Gurukul	A traditional Hindu school.
Hartal	Cessation of work; Strike.
Hundis	A bill of exchange,
Jagir	The grant of land.
Jagirdars	Holders of the Jagirs.

Jehad	A Holy war on behalf of the Islam as a religious duty.
Jathas	Groups.
Jihuzors	Sycopbants.
Khaddar	Hand woven coarse cloth.
Lambardar	The head of the village who may hold the office by descent or election.
Mahal	Sub-division of the district or a taluka, yielding revenue according to assessment, and separately assessed for revenue.
Lathis	Long stick some times tipped with metal used as a weapon.
Mir Bakshi	Pay—master general.
Misaldars	Holders of the Sikh *misls*.
Naib	A Deputy.
Nazrana	Present or gift usually from inferior to superior; forced contribution.
Nazim	District Revenue Officer-cum-Judicial Officer.
Panchayats	Committees, traditionally of five members to decide petty disputes among the people.
Paraganas	District; province; a tract of country comprising many villages.
Pathshalas	Schools.
Patwaris	Those who keep all the accounts connected with the land of the one or more villages.
Qiledar	Fort garrison master; fort commandant.
Resaldar	A native military officer in the cavalry.
Roti	Bread.
Sangathan	Organisation.
Sarkar	Government; district.
Satyagraha	Truth force or soul force.
Satyagrahis	Those who believe in truth force.
Sawar	A horseman.
Shastras	The law books or sacred writings of the Hindus.
Shudhi	Purification.
Subas	Provinces.
Swadeshi	Of one's own country; Indigenous.
Swaraj	Self rule; freedom.
Tehsil	Sub-division of a district or estate.

Thanedar	Officer-in-charge of a police out post.
Vazir	The Prime Minister.
Zaildar	An honorary officer in the village.
Zamindar	Landholder; a collector of revenue on behalf of the government.

Select Bibliography

(A) Unpublished Records

(*a*) Proceedings of the Government of India in the Foreign Department 1800-1810 with special reference to the following branches:
Foreign Secret Consultations:
Foreign Political Consultations:

(*b*) *Government of India Proceedings in the Home Department 1842-1844: Home Revenue Department.*

(*c*) *Home Political (Confidential) Proceedings 1907-1930:*

(*i*) A
(*ii*) B.
(*iii*) Deposit.
(*iv*) K.W.

(*d*) *Confidential Reports of the Native Newspapers of Punjab, 1919.*

(B) Published Records, Reports and Proceedings

Census Report (Punjab) 1919.
1941.
1951.

Disorders Enquiry Committee (Hunter) Report, Calcutta 1923.
Disorders Enquiry Committee Evidence, Vols. I-V, Calcutta, 1920.
District Gazetteers (Of Various Districts).

Ambala and Kalsia State (1912).
Gurgaoa (1910).
Hissar and Loharu State (1912).
Karnal (1912).
Rohtak (1912).

Imperial Gazetteer of India, Vol. V, XI, XIII, XV, (First ed., 1909.

Imperial Gazetteer of India, New Delhi, 1971.

Imperial Legislative Council, Proceedings, 1918-1920.

India, 1919-1929, (Published Yearly).

Indian History Congress, Proceedings (Published Yearly).

Indian Round Table Conference, Vol, III, London, 1932.

Legislative Department, Proceedings, 1900.

Lok Sabha Debates, 1961.

Punjab History Conference, Proceedings, 1965-1979.

Punjab Legislative Council, Proceedings, 1917-1921, London.

Report on the Administration of the Punjab and its Dependencies, 1882-83—1923-24.

Report of the Indian National Congress, (1885-1921) (Published yearly).

Report of the Parliamentary Committee on the Demand of the Punjabi Suba, Delhi, 1965.

Report of the Punjab Boundary Commission, 1966.

Report of the Popular Education in the Punjab and its Dependencies, 1866-67, Lahore.

Report of the State Reorganisation Commission, Delhi, 1956.

Selections from the Punjab Govt. Records, Vol. VIII, Lahore, 1911.

Settlement Reports (of various districts), Karnal, Delhi.

(C) Private Papers

A.I.C.C. Papers, 1919-40.

Chelmsford Papers (Microfilm).

Lala Shamlal (of Hissar) Papers.

M.R. Jayakar Diaries.

Neki Ram Sharma Papers.

Neki Ram Sharma Diaries.

(D) Unpublished Thesis, Dissertations and Other Works

Anant, Bir Singh, *Master Tara Singh and the Punjabi Suba*, (Punjabi University, Patiala, 1971-72).

Barrier, N. Gerald, *Punjab Politics and the Disturbances of 1907*, (Duke University, 1966).

Datta, V.N. and Phadake, H.A., *History of the Kurukshetra*, (Kurukshetra, 1979).

Dhar, Banwari Lal, *Haryana Maratha Sambandh*, (Kurukshetra University, Kurukshetra, 1978).

Jagdish Chander, *Freedom Struggle in Haryana*, (1919-1947), (Kurukshetra University, Kurukshetra, 1976).

Kaur, Karanjit, *Akali Dal's Contribution to the Freedom Movement,* (1920-47), (Punjabi University, Patiala, 1978).

Naidis, Mark, *The Punjab Disturbances of 1919; A Study in Nationalism,* (Stanford University, 1950).

Prem Chand, *The Social Reform Movements in Punjab* 1873-1900 (Kurukshetra University, Kurukshetra, 1978).

Sharma, Inderjeet, *Government and Politics in Haryana* (1797-1803), (Kurukshetra University, Kurukshetra, 1977).

Sulankhi, Balwan Singh, *Swami Shraddhanand,* (Kurukshetra University, Kurukshetra, 1978).

(E) Journals, Periodicals and Newspapers

Calcutta Review (Calcutta) 1849.

Haryana Review (Chandigarh) 1968-1979.

Islamic Culture (Hyderabad) 1934.

Jan Sahitya (Chandigarh) 1971-1979.

Journal of Indian History (Trivendrum) 1961-1979.

Journal of Haryana Studies (Kurukshetra) 1969-1979.

Kurukshetra University Research Journal, (Kurukshetra) 1967-79.

The Hindu (Madras) 1884.

The Hindustan Times (Delhi) 1932.

The Panjabee (Lahore) 1904-11.

The People (Lahore) 1925-29.

The Spokesman (Delhi) 1961.

The Tribune (Lahore, now at Chandigarh), 1881-1947, 1977.

(F) Books

Agnihotri, H.L. and S.N. Malik, *A Profile in Courage, A Biography of Ch. Chhotu Ram,* Delhi, 1978.

Ahmad, Q., *The Wahabi Movement in India,* Calcutta, 1966.

Aitchison , C.U. (Comp.), *A Collection of Treaties Engagements and Sanads relating to India and Neighbouring Countries,* Vols. III-V, Calcutta, 1932.

Allan, J.,W. Haig and H.H. Dodwell, *The Cambridge Shorter History of India,* New York, 1934.

Amba Prasad, *The Revolt of 1942,* Delhi, 1958.

Andrews, C.F. and Girija K., Mukherjee, *The Rise and Growth of Congress in India,* London, 1938.

Argov, Daniel, *Moderates and Extremists in the Indian National Movement* (1885-1920), London, 1964.

Bali A.N., *Now it can be Told,* Jullundur, 1949.

Balidan Jyanti Smarti Granth (H), Jullundur, 1962.

Banerjee, *A.C., Peshwa Madho Rao I.*

Banerjee, S.N., *A Nation in Making, The Reminisences of 50 Years of Public Life*, (London, 1925), Calcutta, 1963.

Bagal, J.C., *History of Indian Association*, Calcutta, 1953.

Bhanu, Dharm, *History and Administration of the North-Western* Provinces (1803-1858).

Bhargava, K.D. (Ed.), *Browne Correspondence*, New Delhi, 1960.

Bipin Chandra, *Nationalism and Colonialism in Modern India*, Delhi, 1979,

Bisheshwar Prasad (Ed.), *Ideas in History*, Bombay, 1968.

Bose, S.C., *The Indian Struggle*, Bombay, 1964.

Breacher, Michael, *Nehru A Political Biography*, London, 1959.

Browne, *India Tracts*, 2 Vols., London, 1788.

Brown, J. Cave, *The Punjab and Delhi in 1857*, 2 Vols., Edinburgh, 1861.

Buddha Prakash, *Haryana Through the Ages*, Kurukhshetra, 1970.

—, *Glimpses of Haryana*, Kurukshetra, New Delhi.

Calendar of Persian Correspondent (1757-1787), *Vols. II, IV, VI*, Delhi, 1940-58.

Calvert, H., *Wealth and Welfare of the Punjab*, Lahore, 1922.

Chandravarkar, Prof., *Maha Punjab*, Hoshiarpur, 1954.

Chaudhry, S.B., *Civil Disturbances During the British Rule in India*, 1765-1857, Calcutta, 1955.

—, *Growth of Nationalism in India*, New Delhi, 1973.

Chirol, Valentine, *India*, London, 1926.

Chopra, Prabha, *Delhi History and Places of Interest*, Delhi, 1970.

Chopra, P.N. (Ed.), *Quit India Movement: British Secret Paper*, Faridabad, 1976.

Compton, Harbert, *A Particular Account of the European Military Adventurers of Hindostan from 1784-1803*. (First ed. 1892), Karachi, 1976.

Cooper, Frederic, *Crisis in Punjab from the 10th May Until the Fail of Delhi*, London, 1858.

Coupland, R., *The Constitutional Problem in India*, Oxford, 1944.

Cunningham, J.D., *A History of the Sikhs from Origin of the Nation to the Battle of the Sutlej*, (First ed. 1849), Delhi, 1972.

Curzon, Lord, *Speeches*, 4 Vols. Calcutta, 1906.

Darbara Singh, *The Punjab Tragedy*, Amritsar, 1949.

Datta, V.N., *Jallianwala Bagh*, Ludhiana, 1969.

Desai, T.B., *Economic History of India Under the British*.

Desraj, *Punjab Ka Itihas* (H), Sangaria, 1954.

Duff, J. Grant, *History of the Marathas*, 3 Vols., (First ed. 1826), Allahabad, 1965.

Duni Chand, *The Ulster of India*, Lahore, 1936.

Dutta, R.C., Economic *History of India in the Victorian Age*, London, 1950.

Edwards, Michael, *King of the World: The Life and Times of Shah Alam Emperor of Hindustan*, London, 1970.

Elliot, H.M. and John Downson, *The History of India as told by its Historians*, Vol. viii, Allahabad, 1964.

Farooqi, *British Relations with the cis-Sutlej States 1809-1823*, Punjab Govt. Monograph No. 19, Lahore, n.d.

Forester, George, *Travels: A Journey from Bengal to England*' 2 Vols., (First Ed. London, 1798), Patiala, 1970.

Fort-William-India House Correspondence 1770-72, (Ed. Bisheshwar Prasad), Vol. VI, NAI, Delhi, I960.

—, *1782-86*, (Ed. C.H. Philips and B.B. Misra), Vol. XV, NAI, Delhi, 1963.

—, *1787-1791*, (Ed. Askari Syed Hasan), Vol. XVI, NAI, Delhi, 1976.

—, *1796-1800*, (Ed. Heras. Rev. Father, H.) Vol. XVIII, NAI, Delhi, 1974.

—, *1792-1796*, (Ed. A.C. Banerjee) Vols. XX, NAI, Delhi, 1969.

Francklin, W., *The History of the Region of Shah Allum*, (First Ed. London, 1803), Allahabad, 1915.

Gadgil, D.R., *The Industrial Evolution of India in Recent Times*, Calcutta, 1950.

Ganda Singh, *Ahmad Shah Durrani*, Bombay, 1959.

—, *Private Correspondence relating to the Anglo-Sikh Wars*, Amritsar, 1955.

Gardhi, M.K., *The Story of my Experiments with Truth*, Ahmedabad, 1963.

—, *The Collected Works of M.K. Gandhi*, Vol. XVIII, XIV, Delhi, 1965.

Gauba, K.L., *The Hon'ble Sir Shadi Lal*, Lahore, 1945.

—, *The Rebel Minister: The Story of the Rise and Fall of Lala Harkishan Lal*, Lahore, 1938.

Ghosh, P.C., *Mahatma Gandhi as I saw him*, Delhi, 1968.

Gopal, S., *Jawaharlal Nehru's Biography*, Vol. I, Delhi, 1976.

Griffin, L.H., *The Rajas of the Punjab*, Lahore, 1870.

Griffin and Massey, *The Punjab Chiefs and Families of Note*, 2 Vols., Lahore 1888.

Grover, B.L., *A Documentary Study of British Policy Towards Indian Nationalism*, Delhi, 1969.

Gupta, Ghanshyam Singh; *The Case of Arya Samaj and Régional Language Formula in Punjab*, Delhi, n.d.

Gupta, H.R., *Studies in Later Mughal History of the Punjab*, Lahore, 1944.

Gurumukh Nihal Singh, *Landmarks in Indian Constitutional and National Movement*, Delhi, 1963.

Gurukul Kangri Ke Sath Varsha, Haridwar, 1960.

Haiq, Sir W., *The Cambridge History of India*, Vol. IV, Delhi, 1957.

Hebber, Reginald, *Narrative of Journey through the Upper Provinces of India*, Vol. II, London, 1829.

Heimsath, C.H., *Indian Nationalism and Hindu Social Reform*, Princeton, 1964.

Hunter, Sir W.W., *The Indian Musalmans*, Calcutta, 1876.

Husain, Azim, *Fazl-i-Husain, A Political Biography, Bombay*, 1946.

Husain, Mahadi, *Balladur Shah II and the War of 1857 in, Delhi*, Delhi, 1958.

Hutchins, Francis G., *Spontaneous Revolution: The Quit India Movement*, Delhi, 1971.

Irving, Miles, *List of Inscriptions on Tombs and Monuments in the Punjab, N.W.F. Province, Kashmir and Afghanistan*, Vol. II,Lahore, 1910.

Javed, R.C., *Punjab Ka Arya Samaj* (H), Jullundur, 1964.

Jha, Manoranjan, *Civil Disobedience Movement and After*, Meerut, 1973.

Josh, Bhagwan, *Communist Movement in Punjab 1926-1947*, Delhi, 1979.

Joshi, Sadhu Ram, *Insanyat Ke Pehredar* (H), New Delhi, 1972.

Joshi, V.C., Lajpat Rai—*A Biographical Eassay*, Delhi, 1966.

—(Ed.), *Lajpat Rai Writings and Speeches*, 2 Vols., Delhi, 1965.

Juneja, M.M., *Neki Ram Sharma and the Freedom Movement*, Hissar, 1979.

Karunkaran, P., *Religion and Political Awakening in India*, Meerut. 1965.

Kaye, Sir John William, *Life of Lord Metcalfe*, 2 Vols., London, 1854.

—, *Selections from the Papers of Charles Metcalfe*, London, 1845.

—, *A History of the Sepoy War in India* (1857-63), Vol. II, London, 1878.

Keen, H.G., *The Fall of the Mughal Empire: An Historical Essay Being a new edition of the Moghal Empire from the death of Aurangzeb*, (First ed. 1876), Delhi, 1971.

Keith, A.B., *The Constitutional History of India*, Allahabad, 1961.

Kincaid, C.A., *A History of the Maratha People*, London, 1931.

Khushwant Singh, *A History of the Sikhs*, 2 Vols, Princeton, 1966.

Lajpat Rai, *The Arya Samaj*, London, 1915.

—, *Young India: An Interpretation and A History of the Nationalist Movement from Within*, Lahore, 1927.

Latif, Syed Muhammed, *History of the Punjab, from the Remotest Antiquity to the Present Time*, (First ed. 1890), New Delhi, 1964.

Leigh, M.S., *The Punjab and the War*, Lahore, 1922.

Leitner, G.W., *History of Indigenous Education in the Punjab since Annexation and in 1882*, Patiala, 1978.

Loharu Kand Ushke Karan Aur Ilaj, (H) Bhiwahi, n.d.

Low, D.A. (Ed.), *Soundings in Modern South Asian History*, London, 1968.

MacDonald, Ramsay, *The Government of India*, London, 1919.

Major, E., *Viscount Morley and Indian Reform*, London, 1910.

Majumdar, A.C., *India National Evolution, A Brief Survey of the Origin and Progress of the Indian National Congress and the Growth of Indian Nationalism*, New Delhi, 1974.

Majumdar, J.K., *Indian Speeches and Documents on British Policy*, Calcutta, 1937.

Majumdar R.C., *The Sepoy Mutiny and Revolt* of 1857, Calcutta, 1963.

—, *The Maratha Supermacy*, Bombay, 1977.

—, *History of the Freedom Movement in India*, Vol. I, Calcutta 1971.

Malleson, Lt. Col. G.B., *The Red Pamphlet* (*The Mutiny of the Bengal Army*), London, 1858.

Malley, L.S.S.O. (Ed.), *Modern India and the West*, Oxford, 1968.

Martin, Briton., *New India 1885*, Oxford, 1970.

Marx, K. and Engles, *The First Indian War of Independence, (1857-59)*, Moscow, 1975.

Mehrotra, S.R., *The Emergence of the Indian National Congress* Delhi, 1971.

Mehta, H.R., *A History of the Growth and Development of Western Education in the Punjab 1846-1884*, (First ed. 1930), Patiala 1971.

Mill, J., *History of British India*, Vol. VII, London 1848.

Mittal. S.C., *Freedom Movement in Punjab, 1905-1929*, Delhi, 1977.

—, *Adhunik Bharat Ka Arthik Itihas* (*H*), Jullundur City, 1976.

—, *Deshratan Lala Lajpat Rai*, (*H*) Saharanpur, 1972.

Minto, Mary (Countess of), India: *Minto and Morley*, London, 1909.

Montgomery, R. Martin, *The History of Indian Empire*, 3 Vols., London, 1961.

Muir, W., *James Thompson Late Lieutenant Governor*, London, 1879.

Muni Lal, *Haryana on the High Road to Prosperity*, Delhi, 1974.

Muztar, B.K., *Kurukshetra : Political and Cultural History*, New Delhi, 1978.

Nair, Sir C. Sankaran, *An Autobiography*, Madras, 1966.

Narain, V.N., *Social History of Modern India*: *Nineteenth Century*, Meerut, 1972.

Nayar, B.R., *Minority, Politics in the Punjab*, Princeton, 1966.

Nehru, J., *Discovery of India*, Calcutta 1946.

—, *An Autobiography*, London, 1958.

Niemeijai, A.C., *The Khilafat Movement in India*, 1919-20, Hague, 1972.

O'Dwyer, Sir Michael, *India As I Knew it* (*1885-1925*), London, 1925.

Oswell, G.D., *Sketches of Rulers of India*: *The Company Governors*, Vol. IL (First ed., 1908), Delhi, 1972.

Pakistan Govt. *A Note on the Sikh Plan, Sikh Plan in Action, Rashtriya Sewamsewek Sangh*, (Pamphlets).

Panjab Government, *One Step Forward: East Punjab Achievement 1948-49, 1950.*

Pandey, D.P., *The Arya Samaj and Indian Nationalism 1875-1920*, New Delhi, 1972.

Pandit Din Dayalu Sharma Satabdi Granth. n.d.

Pandit Din Dayalu Sharma Ka Sanskshift Jiwan Charit, n.d.

Pal, B.C., *Beginning of Freedom Movement in Modern India*, Calcutta, 1954.

Panigrahi, D.N., *Charless Metcalfe in India*, Delhi, 1970.

Panikkar, K.N., *British Diplomacy in North India: A Study of Delhi Residency* (1803-57), New Delhi, 1968.

Parthasarthy, R.S., *A Hundred Years of the Hindu: The Epic Story of Indian Nationalism*, Madras, 1968.

Paul, K.T., *The British Connection with India*, London, 1927.

Peary, Mohan, *An Imaginery Rebellion, how it was Suppressed*, Lahore, 1920.

Philips, C.H. (Ed.), *The Correspondence of Lord William Cavendish Bentinck (1828-1835)*, 2 Vols., Oxford, 1977.

Poona Residence Correspondence (Ed. J.N. Sarkar in English), *1785-1794*, Vol. I, Bombay, 1936.

Powell Price, J.C., *A History of India*, New York, 1958.

Qanungo, K.R., *Historical Essays*, Agra, 1960.

Rai, En Mangat, *Commitment My Style, Career in the Indian Civil Service*, Delhi, 1973.

Rai, Satya M., *Partition of the Punjab*, Bombay, 1965.

Rajendra Prasad, *Autobiography*, Bombay, 1957.

Randhawa, M.S., *Out of the Ashes: An Account of the Rehabilitation of Refugees from West Pakistan in Rural Areas of East Punjab*, Jullundur, 1954.

Ranjit Singh, *Haryana Ke Arya Samaj Ka Itihas*, (H), Rohtak, Vikrimi 2033.

Ravinder Kumar (Ed.), *Essays on Gandhian Politics: The Rowlatt Satyagraha of 1919*, Oxford, 1971.

Rizvi, S.A.A., *Swantra Delhi* (H), Varanasi, 1957.

Sardesai, G.S., *The Main Currents of Maratha History*, Bombay, 1933.

Sarkar, Jagdish Narain, *A Study of Eighteenth Century India*, Vol. I (Political), Calcutta, 1976.

Sarkar, Jadu Nath, *Fall of the Mughal Empire*, Vols. II, III, IV, Calcutta, First Ed. 1934-1950, 1971-72.

Sen, S.N., E*ighteen Fifty Seven*, Delhi, 1957.

Sharda, H.B., *Life of Dayanand Saraswati*, Ajmer, 1946.

Sharma, Jagdish S., *India's Struggle for Freedom, Selected, Documents and Soures*, 3 Vols., Delhi, 1962-65.

Sharma, Ramvilas, *Sun Satavan Ki Kranti* (H), Agra, 1957.

Sharma, S.R., *The Crescent in India*, Bombay, 1934.

—, *Punjab in Ferment*, Delhi, 1971.

Sharma, Shri Ram, *Haryana Ke Nav Rattan* (H), Rohtak, 1978.

—, *Meri Apni Ram Kahani* (H), Rohtak, 1977.

—, *Haryana Ka Itihas* (H), Rohtak, 1974.

Sharp, *Selections from Educational Record*, Vol. I, Delhi, 1965.

Shastri, Algu Rai, *Lajpat Rai*, Prayag, 1957.

Sindhu, Virendra, *Yugdarshta Bhagat Singh aur unke Mirtungya Purkhe* (H), Varanasi, 1968.

Sinha, N.K., *Rise of the Sikh Power*, Calcutta, 1960.

Sitaramayya, Pattabhi, *History of the Indian National Congress*, Vol. I, Delhi, 1965.

Smith, Bosworth, *The Life of Lord Lawrence*, London, 1883.

Smith, V.A., The *Oxford History of India*, Oxford, 1923, 1957.

Spear, Percival, *Twilight of the Mughals*, Cambridge, 1951.

Stephens Ian, *Pakistan*, London, 1963.

Sulug, H.D., *Pt. Neki Ram Sharma Abhinanda Granth*, Calcutta, 1953.

Sunderlal Pandit, *Bharat Men Angrezi Raj Ke Do So Varsh* (H); Delhi, 1960.

Talib, Gurcharan Singh and Lal Singh Giani, *Idea of the Sikh State*, London, n.d.

Tandulkar, D.G., *Mahatma* (*Life of Mohandas Karam Chand Gandhi*), Vol. II, Delhi, 1961.

Tara Chand, *History of the Freedom Movement in India*, Vol. II, & IV, Delhi, 1967.

Teja Singh, *History of Haryana*, New Delhi, 1974.

Temple, Richard, *James Thomson* (Rulers of India Series), London, 1879.

Upadhaya, G.P., *The Origin, Scope and Mission of the Arya Samaj*, Allahabad, 1954.

Vidyalankar, Jay Chand, *The Language and Script Problem in the Punjab*, Jullundur, 1966.

Vidyalankar, S.S., *Jiwan Sangarsh* (H), Delhi, 1964.

Yadav, K.C. *The Revolt of 1857 in Haryana*, New Delhi, 1977.

—, (Ed.). *Haryana Studies in History and Culture*, Kurukshetra, 1968.

Wasti, Syed Razi, *Lord Minto and the Indian National Movement*, Oxford, 1964.

Zaidi, A. Moin, *The Way Out of Freedom*: *An Inquiry into the Quit India Movement conducted by Participants*, Delhi, 1973.

Index

C

K

Q

R

S

T

U

V

W

Y

Z